Spring Framework Essentials

Mastering Spring Framework for Building Effective Java Applications

Thompson Carey

Table of Contents

Preface

Hello, fellow coder! If you're holding this book, chances are you're looking to get a solid grip on the Spring Framework. And you've come to the right place. Let's be honest, Spring can seem a bit...intimidating at first. All those modules, configurations, and concepts can feel like navigating a maze. But don't worry, we're going to break it all down, step by step, and make it feel like you're chatting with a friend over coffee.

Background and Motivation

I remember when I first started with Spring. It felt like trying to learn a new language while building a house. There were so many pieces, and figuring out how they fit together was a real challenge. I spent countless hours sifting through documentation and trying to piece together examples. That's why I wrote this book. I wanted to create a resource that cuts through the noise and provides a clear, practical guide to the essentials. I wanted to share what I learned, the shortcuts, and the best practices, so you don't have to struggle as much as I did.

Purpose and Scope

This book is designed to give you a strong foundation in the core aspects of the Spring Framework. We'll start with the basics, like Dependency Injection and configuration, and then move on to building web applications, working with databases, creating RESTful services, and testing. We'll also cover Spring Boot, which simplifies a lot of the setup and configuration. My goal is to equip you with the knowledge and skills you need to build effective, robust Java applications using Spring.

Target Audience

This book is for anyone who wants to learn Spring. Whether you're a beginner just starting out with Java development or an experienced programmer looking to add Spring to your toolkit, you'll find valuable information here. We'll focus on practical examples and real-world scenarios, so you can see how these concepts apply to actual projects.

Organization and Structure

We've organized the book into three main parts. First, we'll cover the foundational concepts, like Dependency Injection and configuration. Then, we'll move on to building real-world applications using Spring MVC, data access, and RESTful services. Finally, we'll touch on advanced topics like Spring Boot and best practices for building scalable and maintainable applications. Each chapter builds on the previous one, so you can gradually increase your understanding and confidence.

Invitation to Read

So, grab a cup of your favorite beverage, get comfortable, and let's get started. I'm excited to guide you through the essentials of the Spring Framework. By the time you finish this book, you'll have the skills and knowledge to build powerful Java applications with Spring. Let's make learning Spring an enjoyable and rewarding experience!

Chapter 1: Getting Started with Spring - Your Foundation

You're here because you want to understand the Spring Framework, right? Fantastic! Think of this chapter as laying the groundwork. We're not going to jump into complex code right away. Instead, we'll build a solid understanding of what Spring is, why it exists, and how to get your environment ready.

Imagine Spring as a really well-organized workshop. You've got all these tools, components, and frameworks that work together seamlessly. But before you can build anything, you need to know where the tools are, how they work, and how to set up your workspace. That's what we're tackling here.

1.1 What is Spring? History and Evolution

Alright, let's really get into the core of what Spring is, its history, and its evolution, keeping it conversational and detailed, just like we're chatting over coffee.

So, you want to know about Spring, huh? That's great! To understand what it is today, let's rewind a bit. Back in the early 2000s, Java was the king of enterprise application development. But, it wasn't always smooth sailing. Developers were dealing with a lot of complexity, especially with Enterprise JavaBeans (EJBs). Now, EJBs were supposed to simplify things, but they often made them more complex. They were heavy, required a lot of configuration, and were generally a pain to work with.

Rod Johnson, the guy who created Spring, saw this problem. He believed there had to be a simpler, more efficient way to build Java applications. He wrote a book called "Expert One-on-One J2EE Design and Development," and in it, he laid out his vision for a lightweight, modular framework. That book became the blueprint for the Spring Framework.

Initially, Spring was known for its Inversion of Control (IoC) container. Let me explain that a bit. Imagine you're building a house. Traditionally, you'd have to manage all the materials and tools yourself. With IoC, you have a contractor (the Spring container) who manages all that for you. You just tell the contractor what you need, and they provide it. In code terms, this means you don't have to manually create and manage objects. You just tell Spring what objects you need, and it handles the rest. This makes your code cleaner, more modular, and easier to test.

Here's a simple example:

Let's say you have a MessageService that depends on a MessageFormatter.

Without Spring, you might write something like this:

```Java
class MessageFormatter {

    String format(String message) {

        return "Formatted: " + message;

    }

}




class MessageService {

    MessageFormatter formatter = new
MessageFormatter();
```

```java
    void printMessage(String message) {

System.out.println(formatter.format(message));

    }

}


public class Main {

    public static void main(String[] args) {

        MessageService service = new
MessageService();

        service.printMessage("Hello, world!");

    }

}
```

With Spring, you'd do something like this:

```
Java

import org.springframework.stereotype.Component;


@Component

class MessageFormatter {

    String format(String message) {
```

```java
        return "Formatted: " + message;

    }

}


@Component

class MessageService {

    private final MessageFormatter formatter;


    MessageService(MessageFormatter formatter) {

        this.formatter = formatter;

    }


    void printMessage(String message) {

System.out.println(formatter.format(message));

    }

}


// beans.xml

<beans
xmlns="http://www.springframework.org/schema/bean
s"
```

```xml
xmlns:xsi="http://www.w3.org/2001/XMLSchema-insta
nce"

xsi:schemaLocation="http://www.springframework.or
g/schema/beans

http://www.springframework.org/schema/beans/sprin
g-beans.xsd">


    <bean id="messageFormatter"
class="MessageFormatter"/>

    <bean id="messageService"
class="MessageService">

        <constructor-arg ref="messageFormatter"/>

    </bean>


</beans>
```

```java
// Main.java

import
org.springframework.context.ApplicationContext;

import
org.springframework.context.support.ClassPathXmlA
pplicationContext;
```

```java
public class Main {

    public static void main(String[] args) {

        ApplicationContext context = new
ClassPathXmlApplicationContext("beans.xml");

        MessageService service =
context.getBean(MessageService.class);

        service.printMessage("Hello, Spring!");

    }

}
```

See the difference? We're not creating the MessageFormatter inside MessageService. Instead, we're telling Spring to inject it. This makes our code more decoupled and easier to test.

But Spring didn't stop there. It grew into a massive ecosystem. Think of it like a set of building blocks. You have Spring MVC for building web applications, Spring Data for working with databases, Spring Security for securing your applications, and Spring Boot for simplifying configuration.

Spring MVC, for example, is a module that helps you build web applications using the Model-View-Controller (MVC) pattern. It handles things like routing requests, processing forms, and rendering views.

Spring Data simplifies database access. It provides abstractions for working with different databases, so you don't have to write a lot of boilerplate code.

Spring Security handles authentication and authorization. It provides a comprehensive set of security features, so you can protect your applications from unauthorized access.

And then there's Spring Boot, which is a game-changer. It takes a lot of the boilerplate configuration out of Spring and makes it easy to get started with new projects. With Spring Boot, you can create a production-ready Spring application with just a few lines of code.

Here's a real-world example:

Imagine you're building an e-commerce website. You'd use Spring MVC to handle the web requests, Spring Data to manage the product and customer data, and Spring Security to protect the user accounts. Spring Boot would tie it all together and make it easy to deploy.

The evolution of Spring is a testament to its adaptability and usefulness. It went from a simple IoC container to a comprehensive platform for building all kinds of Java applications. And it's still evolving, with new features and improvements being added all the time.

So, that's Spring in a nutshell. It's a powerful and versatile framework that can help you build robust and scalable Java applications. And as we move through this book, we'll explore all these modules in more detail.

1.2 Setting Up Your Development Environment

Alright, let's talk about setting up your development environment for Spring. This is a crucial step, and I want to make sure you get it right from the start. Think of it like preparing your workshop before starting a big project. You need the right tools and a clean workspace to make things run smoothly.

First things first, you'll need the Java Development Kit, or JDK. This is the foundation of any Java project, including Spring applications. The JDK allows you to compile and run Java code. You can get the latest JDK from Oracle's website or use an open-source distribution like OpenJDK. When you download it, make sure you pick the version that's compatible with your operating system.

After you install the JDK, you need to set the JAVA_HOME environment variable. This tells your system where the JDK is located. On Windows, you can do this by going to System Properties, clicking on Environment Variables, and adding a new variable called JAVA_HOME with the path to your JDK installation. On macOS or Linux, you can set it in your .bash_profile or .zshrc file. This is important because many tools, like Maven or Gradle, rely on this variable.

Now, let's talk about your Integrated Development Environment, or IDE. An IDE is like a supercharged text editor that makes coding much easier. It provides features like code completion, debugging, and project management. There are a few popular IDEs you can choose from, like IntelliJ IDEA, Eclipse, and VS Code. Personally, I prefer IntelliJ IDEA for Spring development, but feel free to use whichever one you're comfortable with.

IntelliJ IDEA, for example, has excellent support for Spring. It provides features like code completion for Spring annotations, refactoring tools, and integration with build tools like Maven and Gradle. Eclipse also has good Spring support, especially with the Spring Tool Suite (STS) plugin. VS Code, with the right extensions, can also be a powerful IDE for Spring development.

Here's a real-world example:

Let's say you are building a web application. An IDE makes it easier to navigate through your project files, write code, and debug any issues that arise. It makes your development process more efficient.

Next, you'll need a build tool. Maven or Gradle are the two most popular build tools for Java projects. They help you manage dependencies, compile code, and run tests. For now, let's focus on Maven. Maven uses a file called pom.xml to define your project's dependencies and build configuration.

Here's a basic pom.xml example:

```xml
XML

<project
xmlns="http://maven.apache.org/POM/4.0.0"


xmlns:xsi="http://www.w3.org/2001/XMLSchema-insta
nce"


xsi:schemaLocation="http://maven.apache.org/POM/4
.0.0

http://maven.apache.org/xsd/maven-4.0.0.xsd">

    <modelVersion>4.0.0</modelVersion>


    <groupId>com.example</groupId>

    <artifactId>my-spring-app</artifactId>

    <version>1.0-SNAPSHOT</version>
```

```xml
<dependencies>

    <dependency>

<groupId>org.springframework</groupId>

<artifactId>spring-context</artifactId>

        <version>5.3.27</version>

    </dependency>

</dependencies>


<build>

    <plugins>

        <plugin>

<groupId>org.apache.maven.plugins</groupId>

<artifactId>maven-compiler-plugin</artifactId>

        <version>3.8.1</version>

        <configuration>

            <source>11</source>

            <target>11</target>

        </configuration>
```

```
        </plugin>

      </plugins>

    </build>

</project>
```

This pom.xml file tells Maven that your project depends on the spring-context library, which is the core of the Spring Framework. Maven will automatically download this library and any other dependencies you specify.

To run Maven commands, you'll need to install it on your system. You can download it from the Apache Maven website. Once installed, you can run commands like mvn compile to compile your code, mvn test to run tests, and mvn package to build a JAR file.

Here's a practical exercise:

Create a simple Maven project in your IDE and add the spring-context dependency. Then, try running the mvn compile command to see if it works. This will help you get comfortable with Maven and ensure your environment is set up correctly.

Setting up your development environment is like preparing your tools before building something. It's a crucial step that will make your development process smoother and more efficient. Take your time, get it right, and you'll be well on your way to building great Spring applications.

1.3 Your First Spring Application: "Hello, Spring!"

Alright, let's get our hands dirty and build our first Spring application. Don't worry, we'll keep it simple: a classic "Hello,

Spring!" program. This will give you a taste of how Spring works and lay the foundation for more complex applications later on.

Think of this as your first step in understanding the Spring container, the heart of the Spring Framework. We'll be using this container to manage our objects, or "beans," as Spring calls them.

First, let's create a new Maven project. If you're using IntelliJ IDEA, you can create a new Maven project from the "New Project" wizard. Make sure you select the maven-archetype-quickstart archetype, which gives you a basic project structure.

Now, we need to add the Spring Context dependency to our pom.xml file. This dependency provides the core functionality of the Spring container.

Here's how your pom.xml should look:

XML

```xml
<project
xmlns="http://maven.apache.org/POM/4.0.0"


xmlns:xsi="http://www.w3.org/2001/XMLSchema-insta
nce"


xsi:schemaLocation="http://maven.apache.org/POM/4
.0.0


http://maven.apache.org/xsd/maven-4.0.0.xsd">

    <modelVersion>4.0.0</modelVersion>
```

```xml
<groupId>com.example</groupId>

<artifactId>hello-spring</artifactId>

<version>1.0-SNAPSHOT</version>


<dependencies>

    <dependency>

<groupId>org.springframework</groupId>

<artifactId>spring-context</artifactId>

        <version>5.3.27</version>

    </dependency>

</dependencies>


<build>

    <plugins>

        <plugin>

<groupId>org.apache.maven.plugins</groupId>

<artifactId>maven-compiler-plugin</artifactId>

            <version>3.8.1</version>
```

```xml
            <configuration>

                <source>11</source>

                <target>11</target>

            </configuration>

        </plugin>

    </plugins>

</build>

</project>
```

Next, let's create a simple Java class. We'll call it HelloWorld.java. This class will contain our main method and the logic to retrieve our message from the Spring container.

Java

```java
import
org.springframework.context.ApplicationContext;

import
org.springframework.context.support.ClassPathXmlA
pplicationContext;


public class HelloWorld {

    public static void main(String[] args) {

        ApplicationContext context = new
ClassPathXmlApplicationContext("beans.xml");
```

```java
        String message = (String)
context.getBean("message");

        System.out.println(message);

    }

}
```

Now, let's create our beans.xml file. This file is where we define our Spring beans. A bean is simply an object that's managed by the Spring container. In this case, we'll define a bean of type String with the message "Hello, Spring!".

Create a file called beans.xml in the src/main/resources folder.

XML

```xml
<?xml version="1.0" encoding="UTF-8"?>

<beans
xmlns="http://www.springframework.org/schema/bean
s"


xmlns:xsi="http://www.w3.org/2001/XMLSchema-insta
nce"


xsi:schemaLocation="http://www.springframework.or
g/schema/beans


http://www.springframework.org/schema/beans/sprin
g-beans.xsd">


    <bean id="message" class="java.lang.String">
```

```
    <constructor-arg value="Hello, Spring!"
/>

  </bean>


</beans>
```

Let's break down what's happening here. In beans.xml, we're defining a bean with the id "message" and the class java.lang.String. We're also passing the value "Hello, Spring!" to the constructor of the String class.

In HelloWorld.java, we're creating an ApplicationContext, which is the Spring container. We're using ClassPathXmlApplicationContext to load our beans from the beans.xml file. Then, we're retrieving the bean with the id "message" and printing it to the console.

Now, run the HelloWorld.java class. You should see "Hello, Spring!" printed to the console.

This is a simple example, but it demonstrates the basic principles of Spring. We're using the Spring container to manage our objects and inject dependencies.

Here's a practical exercise:

Try changing the message in beans.xml and running the application again. You should see the new message printed to the console. This will help you understand how Spring loads and manages your beans.

Here's a real-world example:

Let's say you're building a web application. You might have a UserService that depends on a UserRepository. Instead of creating the UserRepository inside the UserService, you can define them as beans in your Spring configuration and let Spring inject them. This makes your code more modular and easier to test.

Remember, this is just the beginning. As we progress through this book, we'll explore more advanced Spring concepts and build more complex applications. But understanding the basics is crucial. So, take your time, experiment with the code, and don't hesitate to ask questions.

Chapter 2: Dependency Injection (DI)

So, you've heard about Dependency Injection, right? It's a big deal in Spring, and for good reason. It's a design pattern that helps you write cleaner, more modular, and more testable code. In simple terms, it's about giving an object its dependencies instead of having the object create them itself.

2.1 Understanding Dependency Injection

Alright, let's really unpack Dependency Injection (DI) and get a solid understanding of what it is and why it's so important in Spring.

So, you've probably heard the term "Dependency Injection" thrown around a lot, right? It might sound a bit technical, but the concept is actually quite straightforward. In essence, DI is a design pattern that helps you create objects in a way that makes your code more flexible, maintainable, and testable.

To understand DI, let's first talk about what a "dependency" is. In programming, a dependency is simply an object that another object needs to function. For example, if you have a UserService that needs to access data from a database, the UserService depends on a UserRepository. The UserRepository is a dependency of the UserService.

Now, without DI, you might create the UserRepository object inside the UserService.

Here's what that might look like:

Java

```java
class UserRepository {
```

```java
    String getData() {

        return "Data from database";

    }

}


class UserService {

    private UserRepository userRepository = new
UserRepository();


    String getUserData() {

        return userRepository.getData();

    }

}


public class Main {

    public static void main(String[] args) {

        UserService userService = new
UserService();


System.out.println(userService.getUserData());

    }

}
```

In this example, the UserService creates its own UserRepository. This works, but it has a few problems. First, it makes the UserService tightly coupled to the UserRepository. If you want to use a different repository, you have to change the UserService code. Second, it makes the UserService hard to test. To test it properly, you'd have to use a real database, which can be slow and unreliable.

With DI, you'd pass the UserRepository to the UserService instead of creating it inside. This is called "injecting" the dependency.

Here's what that looks like:

```java
Java

class UserRepository {

    String getData() {

        return "Data from database";

    }

}



class UserService {

    private UserRepository userRepository;


    UserService(UserRepository userRepository) {

        this.userRepository = userRepository;

    }
```

```java
    String getUserData() {

        return userRepository.getData();

    }

}


public class Main {

    public static void main(String[] args) {

        UserRepository userRepository = new
UserRepository();

        UserService userService = new
UserService(userRepository);

System.out.println(userService.getUserData());

    }

}
```

In this example, the UserService takes a UserRepository as a constructor argument. This means that the UserService doesn't care where the UserRepository comes from. It just knows that it needs one. This makes the UserService more flexible and easier to test.

Here's a real-world example:

Imagine you're building an e-commerce application. You might have a OrderService that depends on a PaymentGateway. Without

DI, the OrderService might create its own PaymentGateway. But what if you want to use a different payment gateway? With DI, you can simply pass the PaymentGateway to the OrderService, making it easy to switch between different payment gateways.

Now, you might be thinking, "Why not just use a factory pattern?" That's a good question. A factory pattern is similar to DI in that it creates objects, but it's different in a few key ways. With a factory pattern, the object still has to ask for its dependencies from the factory. With DI, the dependencies are pushed into the object.

Here's an exercise to help solidify your understanding:

Try refactoring a piece of code that creates its own dependencies to use DI instead. This will help you see the benefits of DI firsthand.

Dependency Injection is a powerful design pattern that helps you write cleaner, more modular, and more testable code. By passing dependencies to objects instead of creating them inside, you make your code more flexible and easier to maintain. And in Spring, the IoC container handles all this for you, making it even easier to use.

2.2 Constructor Injection

Alright, let's talk about Constructor Injection. This is one of the primary ways we implement Dependency Injection in Spring, and it's generally considered the preferred method. So, what is it, and why is it so useful?

Constructor Injection is all about providing the dependencies an object needs through its constructor. Think of it like this: when you create a new object, you're also providing it with all the ingredients it needs to function right from the start. This makes the object fully initialized and ready to go as soon as it's created.

Let's illustrate this with an example. Suppose we have a ReportGenerator that depends on a DataSource to fetch data.

Without Constructor Injection, you might end up with something like this:

```Java
class DataSource {

    String fetchData() {

        return "Data from source";

    }

}



class ReportGenerator {

    private DataSource dataSource;


    ReportGenerator() {

        this.dataSource = new DataSource();

    }


    String generateReport() {

        return "Report: " +
dataSource.fetchData();

    }

}
```

```java
public class Main {

    public static void main(String[] args) {

        ReportGenerator generator = new
ReportGenerator();


System.out.println(generator.generateReport());

    }

}
```

In this code, the ReportGenerator creates its own DataSource instance. This leads to tight coupling – the ReportGenerator is directly tied to a specific DataSource implementation. If we want to use a different data source, we'd have to modify the ReportGenerator class itself, which isn't ideal.

Now, let's refactor this using Constructor Injection:

```java
Java

class DataSource {

    String fetchData() {

        return "Data from source";

    }

}



class ReportGenerator {
```

```java
    private DataSource dataSource;


    ReportGenerator(DataSource dataSource) {

        this.dataSource = dataSource;

    }


    String generateReport() {

        return "Report: " +
dataSource.fetchData();

    }

}


public class Main {

    public static void main(String[] args) {

        DataSource dataSource = new DataSource();

        ReportGenerator generator = new
ReportGenerator(dataSource);

System.out.println(generator.generateReport());

    }

}
```

In this version, the ReportGenerator takes a DataSource as a constructor argument. This means the ReportGenerator doesn't care *how* the DataSource is created; it just needs one to function. This makes the ReportGenerator more flexible and easier to test.

Here's how you'd configure this in Spring using XML:

XML

```
<beans
xmlns="http://www.springframework.org/schema/bean
s"


xmlns:xsi="http://www.w3.org/2001/XMLSchema-insta
nce"


xsi:schemaLocation="http://www.springframework.or
g/schema/beans


http://www.springframework.org/schema/beans/sprin
g-beans.xsd">


    <bean id="dataSource" class="DataSource"/>

    <bean id="reportGenerator"
class="ReportGenerator">

        <constructor-arg ref="dataSource"/>

    </bean>


</beans>
```

And here's how you'd do it using Java configuration:

```java
Java

import
org.springframework.context.annotation.Bean;

import
org.springframework.context.annotation.Configurat
ion;


@Configuration

public class AppConfig {


    @Bean

    public DataSource dataSource() {

        return new DataSource();

    }


    @Bean

    public ReportGenerator
reportGenerator(DataSource dataSource) {

        return new ReportGenerator(dataSource);

    }

}
```

With Spring, the IoC container takes care of creating and injecting the DataSource into the ReportGenerator. This makes our code even cleaner and more decoupled.

A real-world example:

Imagine you're building a service that sends emails. This service might depend on an email client. Using Constructor Injection, you'd pass the email client to the service through its constructor. This allows you to easily swap out different email clients for testing or production.

Constructor Injection has a few advantages. First, it makes it clear what dependencies an object needs. Second, it ensures that the object is fully initialized when it's created. Third, it makes the object easier to test because you can easily provide mock dependencies.

Here's a small exercise:

Take a class you've written that has dependencies, and refactor it to use Constructor Injection. Then, try writing a unit test for that class, mocking the dependencies. You'll see how much easier testing becomes.

In short, Constructor Injection is a powerful technique that promotes good object-oriented design and makes your code more maintainable and testable. It's a fundamental concept in Spring, and mastering it will significantly improve your Spring development skills.

2.3 Setter Injection

Alright, let's switch gears and talk about Setter Injection. While Constructor Injection is generally preferred, Setter Injection has its place and can be quite useful in certain scenarios. So, what is it, and how does it work?

Setter Injection, as the name suggests, involves providing dependencies to an object through its setter methods. Instead of passing dependencies through the constructor, you use setter methods to inject them after the object has been created. This gives you a bit more flexibility, especially when dealing with optional dependencies.

Let's start with a simple example:

Suppose we have a TextProcessor that can optionally use a SpellChecker to correct the text.

Without Setter Injection, we might have something like this:

Java

```java
class SpellChecker {

    String correct(String text) {

        return text.replaceAll("teh", "the");

    }

}



class TextProcessor {

    private SpellChecker spellChecker;


    TextProcessor(SpellChecker spellChecker) {

        this.spellChecker = spellChecker;
```

```java
    }


    String processText(String text) {

        if (spellChecker != null) {

            return spellChecker.correct(text);

        }

        return text;

    }

}


public class Main {

    public static void main(String[] args) {

        SpellChecker checker = new
SpellChecker();

        TextProcessor processor = new
TextProcessor(checker);

System.out.println(processor.processText("teh
quick brown fox"));

    }

}
```

This works fine when we always need a SpellChecker. But what if we want to create a TextProcessor without a SpellChecker? We'd have to modify the constructor or create a separate constructor without the SpellChecker argument, which can make the code more complex.

Now, let's refactor this using Setter Injection:

Java

```java
class SpellChecker {

    String correct(String text) {

        return text.replaceAll("teh", "the");

    }

}



class TextProcessor {

    private SpellChecker spellChecker;


    void setSpellChecker(SpellChecker
spellChecker) {

        this.spellChecker = spellChecker;

    }


    String processText(String text) {

        if (spellChecker != null) {

            return spellChecker.correct(text);
```

```
        }

        return text;

    }

}


public class Main {

    public static void main(String[] args) {

        TextProcessor processor = new
TextProcessor();

        SpellChecker checker = new
SpellChecker();

        processor.setSpellChecker(checker);


System.out.println(processor.processText("teh
quick brown fox"));

    }

}
```

In this version, we're using a setter method setSpellChecker to inject the SpellChecker. This allows us to create a TextProcessor without a SpellChecker if we want.

Here's how you'd configure this in Spring using XML:

XML

```xml
<beans
xmlns="http://www.springframework.org/schema/bean
s"

xmlns:xsi="http://www.w3.org/2001/XMLSchema-insta
nce"

xsi:schemaLocation="http://www.springframework.or
g/schema/beans

http://www.springframework.org/schema/beans/sprin
g-beans.xsd">


    <bean id="spellChecker"
class="SpellChecker"/>

    <bean id="textProcessor"
class="TextProcessor">

        <property name="spellChecker"
ref="spellChecker"/>

    </bean>


</beans>
```

And here's how you'd do it using Java configuration:

```Java
Java

import
org.springframework.context.annotation.Bean;
```

```java
import
org.springframework.context.annotation.Configurat
ion;


@Configuration

public class AppConfig {


    @Bean

    public SpellChecker spellChecker() {

        return new SpellChecker();

    }


    @Bean

    public TextProcessor textProcessor() {

        return new TextProcessor();

    }


    @Bean

    public void
configureTextProcessor(TextProcessor processor,
SpellChecker checker) {

        processor.setSpellChecker(checker);
```

```
        }

    }
```

With Spring, the IoC container takes care of creating and injecting the SpellChecker into the TextProcessor.

A real-world example:

Imagine you're building a logging system. You might have a LogWriter that can optionally use a Formatter to format the log messages. Using Setter Injection, you can allow the LogWriter to function without a Formatter if needed.

Setter Injection has a few advantages

First, it allows you to inject optional dependencies. Second, it can be useful when you have circular dependencies. However, it also has some drawbacks. It can make it less clear what dependencies an object needs, and it can make the object's state less consistent.

Here's a small exercise:

Take a class you've written that has optional dependencies and refactor it to use Setter Injection. Experiment with creating instances of the class with and without the optional dependencies.

In short, Setter Injection is a useful technique that provides flexibility when dealing with optional dependencies. While Constructor Injection is generally preferred, understanding Setter Injection will give you more tools in your Spring development toolkit.

2.4 Field Injection

Alright, let's talk about Field Injection. This is another way to implement Dependency Injection in Spring, but it's a bit different from Constructor and Setter Injection. While it might seem convenient at first, it's often discouraged in favor of the other two methods. Let's explore why.

Field Injection involves using annotations, specifically @Autowired, to inject dependencies directly into fields. This means you don't need to write constructors or setter methods. Spring's IoC container takes care of injecting the dependencies for you.

Here's an example:

```Java
import
org.springframework.beans.factory.annotation.Auto
wired;



class Logger {

    void log(String message) {

        System.out.println("Log: " + message);

    }

}



class ReportService {

    @Autowired

    private Logger logger;
```

```java
    void generateReport() {

        logger.log("Generating report");

        // ... report generation logic ...

    }

}


public class Main {

    public static void main(String[] args) {

        // Typically, you'd use Spring's
ApplicationContext here

        // But for simplicity, we'll demonstrate
the concept

        ReportService service = new
ReportService();

        service.generateReport();

    }

}
```

In this example, we're using @Autowired to inject the Logger dependency into the ReportService. Spring's IoC container will automatically find a Logger bean and inject it into the logger field.

Herc's how you'd configure this in Spring using XML:

XML

```
<beans
xmlns="http://www.springframework.org/schema/bean
s"

xmlns:xsi="http://www.w3.org/2001/XMLSchema-insta
nce"

xsi:schemaLocation="http://www.springframework.or
g/schema/beans

http://www.springframework.org/schema/beans/sprin
g-beans.xsd">


    <bean id="logger" class="Logger"/>

    <bean id="reportService"
class="ReportService"/>


</beans>
```

And here's how you'd do it using Java configuration:

Java

```
import
org.springframework.context.annotation.Bean;

import
org.springframework.context.annotation.Configurat
ion;
```

```java
@Configuration

public class AppConfig {


    @Bean

    public Logger logger() {

        return new Logger();

    }


    @Bean

    public ReportService reportService() {

        return new ReportService();

    }

}
```

With Spring, the IoC container handles the injection automatically.

Now, you might be thinking, "This seems easy and convenient. Why is it discouraged?" Well, Field Injection has a few drawbacks.

First, it makes your code harder to test. Because the dependencies are injected directly into fields, you can't easily provide mock dependencies in your unit tests. You'd have to use reflection to set the fields, which makes your tests more complex and brittle.

Second, it makes your code less clear. When you use Constructor Injection, it's immediately clear what dependencies an object needs. With Field Injection, you have to look for @Autowired annotations, which can be scattered throughout the class.

Third, it hides dependencies. It makes it harder to understand the object's dependencies just by looking at the class signature. With constructor injection, you know exactly what is needed to construct the object.

Here's a real-world example:

Imagine you're building a service that sends notifications. This service might depend on a notification sender. Using Field Injection, you'd inject the notification sender directly into the service's field. But this would make it harder to test the service in isolation, as you wouldn't be able to easily mock the notification sender.

Here's a small exercise:

Take a class you've written that uses Field Injection and refactor it to use Constructor Injection. Then, try writing unit tests for both versions. You'll see how much easier it is to test the version that uses Constructor Injection.

In short, while Field Injection might seem convenient, it's generally discouraged in favor of Constructor and Setter Injection. Understanding its drawbacks will help you write cleaner, more maintainable, and more testable code.

2.5 Spring's IoC Container and Application Context

Alright, let's talk about the heart of Spring: the IoC container, or more specifically, the Application Context. This is where all the magic of Dependency Injection happens, and understanding it is crucial for building robust Spring applications.

So, what exactly is the IoC container? IoC stands for Inversion of Control. Traditionally, when you write code, you're in control of creating and managing your objects. With IoC, that control is inverted. The container takes over the job of creating and managing your objects, or "beans," as Spring calls them.

Think of the IoC container as a factory. You tell it what objects you need, and it creates them for you. You also tell it how these objects depend on each other, and it wires them together. This way, your objects don't have to worry about creating their dependencies; they just receive them.

In Spring, the IoC container is represented by the ApplicationContext interface. This interface provides methods for accessing and managing your beans. There are several implementations of ApplicationContext, each with its own way of loading bean definitions.

One common implementation is ClassPathXmlApplicationContext. This implementation loads bean definitions from an XML file in your classpath.

Here's an example:

```java
Java

import
org.springframework.context.ApplicationContext;

import
org.springframework.context.support.ClassPathXmlA
pplicationContext;


public class Main {

    public static void main(String[] args) {
```

```java
        ApplicationContext context = new
ClassPathXmlApplicationContext("beans.xml");

        MyService service =
context.getBean(MyService.class);

        service.doSomething();

    }

}
```

In this example, we're creating a ClassPathXmlApplicationContext and passing it the name of our XML file, "beans.xml". The context.getBean() method retrieves a bean from the container.

Here's what our "beans.xml" file might look like:

XML

```xml
<beans
xmlns="http://www.springframework.org/schema/bean
s"


xmlns:xsi="http://www.w3.org/2001/XMLSchema-insta
nce"


xsi:schemaLocation="http://www.springframework.or
g/schema/beans


http://www.springframework.org/schema/beans/sprin
g-beans.xsd">


    <bean id="myService" class="MyService">
```

```xml
        <constructor-arg ref="myRepository"/>

    </bean>


    <bean id="myRepository"
class="MyRepository"/>


</beans>
```

Another common implementation is AnnotationConfigApplicationContext. This implementation loads bean definitions from Java configuration classes.

Here's an example:

```java
Java

import
org.springframework.context.ApplicationContext;

import
org.springframework.context.annotation.Annotation
ConfigApplicationContext;


public class Main {

    public static void main(String[] args) {

        ApplicationContext context = new
AnnotationConfigApplicationContext(AppConfig.clas
s);
```

```java
        MyService service =
context.getBean(MyService.class);

        service.doSomething();

    }

}
```

And here's what our AppConfig class might look like:

```java
Java

import
org.springframework.context.annotation.Bean;

import
org.springframework.context.annotation.Configuration;


@Configuration

public class AppConfig {


    @Bean

    public MyService myService(MyRepository
repository) {

        return new MyService(repository);

    }



    @Bean
```

```
public MyRepository myRepository() {

    return new MyRepository();

}

}
```

The ApplicationContext not only creates and wires beans, but it also provides other features like internationalization, event publishing, and resource loading. It's a central hub for your Spring application.

Here's a real-world example:

Imagine you're building a web application. You might have a UserController that depends on a UserService. With Spring, you can define these beans in your configuration and let the ApplicationContext wire them together. This makes your code more modular and easier to test.

Here's a small exercise:

Create a simple Spring application with two beans and wire them together using either XML or Java configuration. Then, retrieve the beans from the ApplicationContext and use them in your main method. This will help you get comfortable with the ApplicationContext and see how it works.

In short, the Spring IoC container, or ApplicationContext, is a fundamental part of Spring. It takes care of creating and managing your beans, making your code cleaner and more maintainable. Understanding how it works is crucial for building robust Spring applications.

2.6 Bean Scopes and Lifecycles

Alright, let's talk about Bean Scopes and Lifecycles. These concepts are essential for understanding how Spring manages your beans and how you can control their behavior.

First, let's discuss Bean Scopes. When you define a bean in Spring, you're not just defining the class of the object; you're also defining its scope. The scope determines how many instances of the bean are created and how long they live.

The most common scope is singleton. When a bean has a singleton scope, only one instance of that bean is created for the entire Application Context. This is the default scope, and it's suitable for stateless objects like services and repositories.

Here's an example:

XML

```
<bean id="myService" class="MyService"
scope="singleton"/>
```

Or in Java configuration:

Java

```
import
org.springframework.context.annotation.Bean;

import
org.springframework.context.annotation.Configurat
ion;

import
org.springframework.context.annotation.Scope;
```

```java
@Configuration

public class AppConfig {


    @Bean

    @Scope("singleton")

    public MyService myService() {

        return new MyService();

    }

}
```

If you need a new instance of the bean every time it's requested, you can use the prototype scope.

XML

```xml
<bean id="myBean" class="MyBean"
scope="prototype"/>
```

Or in Java configuration:

Java

```java
import
org.springframework.context.annotation.Bean;

import
org.springframework.context.annotation.Configurat
ion;

import
org.springframework.context.annotation.Scope;
```

```
@Configuration

public class AppConfig {


    @Bean

    @Scope("prototype")

    public MyBean myBean() {

        return new MyBean();

    }

}
```

The prototype scope is useful for stateful objects that shouldn't be shared.

In web applications, you'll often encounter the request and session scopes. The request scope creates a new instance of the bean for each HTTP request. The session scope creates a new instance of the bean for each HTTP session.

Here's an example of using the request scope:

XML

```xml
<bean id="myBean" class="MyBean"
scope="request"/>
```

Or in Java configuration:

Java

```java
import
org.springframework.context.annotation.Bean;

import
org.springframework.context.annotation.Configurat
ion;

import
org.springframework.context.annotation.Scope;

import
org.springframework.web.context.WebApplicationCon
text;


@Configuration

public class AppConfig {


    @Bean

    @Scope(WebApplicationContext.SCOPE_REQUEST)

    public MyBean myBean() {

        return new MyBean();

    }

}
```

Now, let's talk about Bean Lifecycles. When a bean is created and managed by the Spring container, it goes through a series of lifecycle events. You can define methods to be called at specific points in the bean's lifecycle.

For example, you can define an initialization method that's called after the bean is created and its dependencies are injected. You can also define a destruction method that's called before the bean is destroyed.

Here's an example:

```Java
class MyBean {

    void init() {

        System.out.println("Initializing bean");

    }


    void destroy() {

        System.out.println("Destroying bean");

    }

}
```

And here's how you'd configure it in XML:

```XML
<bean id="myBean" class="MyBean"
init-method="init" destroy-method="destroy"/>
```

Or in Java configuration:

```Java

```

```java
import
org.springframework.context.annotation.Bean;

import
org.springframework.context.annotation.Configurat
ion;


@Configuration

public class AppConfig {


    @Bean(initMethod = "init", destroyMethod =
"destroy")

    public MyBean myBean() {

        return new MyBean();

    }

}
```

You can also use the @PostConstruct and @PreDestroy annotations to define initialization and destruction methods:

Java

```java
import javax.annotation.PostConstruct;

import javax.annotation.PreDestroy;


class MyBean {

    @PostConstruct
```

```java
void init() {

    System.out.println("Initializing bean");

}


@PreDestroy

void destroy() {

    System.out.println("Destroying bean");

}

}
```

Here's a real-world example:

Imagine you're building a database connection pool. You might want to initialize the connection pool when the bean is created and close the connections when the bean is destroyed.

Here's a small exercise:

Create a Spring application with a bean that has an initialization and a destruction method. Then, run the application and observe the output. This will help you understand how bean lifecycles work.

In short, Bean Scopes and Lifecycles allow you to control how your beans are created and managed by the Spring container. Understanding these concepts is crucial for building robust and efficient Spring applications.

Chapter 3: Spring Configuration

Now, you've probably heard that Spring is all about configuration, right? Well, that's true. But don't worry, it's not as complicated as it might sound. We're going to walk through the different ways you can configure your Spring applications, and by the end of this chapter, you'll be a pro.

3.1 XML-Based Configuration

Let's talk about XML-based configuration in Spring. This was the original, and for a time, the primary way to define beans and their dependencies. While newer methods like Java and annotation-based configurations have gained popularity, understanding XML configuration is still very valuable, especially when you encounter legacy systems or need to work with specific enterprise setups.

So, what exactly is XML-based configuration? It's a method where you define your Spring beans and their relationships using an XML file. This file, traditionally named "beans.xml," is placed within your application's classpath, often in the src/main/resources directory.

Let's start with a basic example. Suppose we have two classes, MessageService and MessageFormatter. The MessageService depends on MessageFormatter to format messages.

We can define these beans and their dependency in an XML file like this:

```
XML

<beans
xmlns="http://www.springframework.org/schema/bean
s"
```

```
xmlns:xsi="http://www.w3.org/2001/XMLSchema-insta
nce"


xsi:schemaLocation="http://www.springframework.or
g/schema/beans


http://www.springframework.org/schema/beans/sprin
g-beans.xsd">


    <bean id="messageFormatter"
class="MessageFormatter"/>


    <bean id="messageService"
class="MessageService">

        <constructor-arg ref="messageFormatter"/>

    </bean>



</beans>
```

In this XML, we're using the `<bean>` element to define our beans. The id attribute gives each bean a unique identifier, and the class attribute specifies the fully qualified class name. For the messageService bean, we're using the `<constructor-arg>` element to inject the messageFormatter bean as a constructor argument. The ref attribute tells Spring to use the bean with the specified ID.

To load this configuration and use the beans, we'd write Java code like this:

Java

```java
import
org.springframework.context.ApplicationContext;

import
org.springframework.context.support.ClassPathXmlA
pplicationContext;


public class Main {

    public static void main(String[] args) {

        ApplicationContext context = new
ClassPathXmlApplicationContext("beans.xml");

        MessageService service =
context.getBean(MessageService.class);

        service.printMessage("Hello, Spring!");

    }

}
```

Here, we're using ClassPathXmlApplicationContext to load the "beans.xml" file from the classpath. Then, we're using context.getBean(MessageService.class) to retrieve the messageService bean from the Spring container.

Now, let's look at a more complex example. Suppose we have a DatabaseService that depends on a DataSource and a TransactionManager.

We can define these beans with properties and constructor arguments:

XML

```xml
<beans
xmlns="http://www.springframework.org/schema/beans"

xmlns:xsi="http://www.w3.org/2001/XMLSchema-instance"

xsi:schemaLocation="http://www.springframework.org/schema/beans

http://www.springframework.org/schema/beans/spring-beans.xsd">


    <bean id="dataSource" class="MyDataSource">

        <property name="url"
value="jdbc:mysql://localhost:3306/mydb"/>

        <property name="username" value="user"/>

        <property name="password"
value="password"/>

    </bean>


    <bean id="transactionManager"
class="MyTransactionManager"/>
```

```
    <bean id="databaseService"
class="DatabaseService">

        <constructor-arg ref="dataSource"/>

        <constructor-arg
ref="transactionManager"/>

    </bean>



</beans>
```

In this case, we're using the <property> element to set properties on the dataSource bean. We're also using multiple <constructor-arg> elements to inject multiple dependencies into the databaseService bean.

A real-world example:

Consider a legacy enterprise application that uses a complex XML configuration to manage its beans. This configuration might involve numerous dependencies, properties, and even AOP aspects. Understanding XML configuration is essential to maintain and extend such an application.

XML configuration also supports features like bean scopes, initialization and destruction methods, and AOP aspects.

For instance, you can define a bean with a prototype scope:

XML

```
<bean id="myBean" class="MyBean"
scope="prototype"/>
```

Or define initialization and destruction methods:

XML

```
<bean id="myBean" class="MyBean"
init-method="init" destroy-method="destroy"/>
```

While XML configuration can be verbose, it's still a powerful tool for defining your Spring beans. Understanding it will give you a solid foundation for working with Spring applications, especially in environments where XML configuration is still prevalent.

Here's an exercise:

Create a simple Spring application with two beans and wire them together using XML configuration. Experiment with different bean scopes and properties. This will help you get comfortable with XML-based configuration and see how it works in practice.

3.2 Java-Based Configuration

Let's move on to Java-based configuration, a more modern and generally preferred approach compared to XML. With Java-based configuration, you define your beans and their dependencies using Java code, which brings several benefits, including improved readability, maintainability, and type safety.

So, how does it work? You use Java classes annotated with @Configuration to define your beans. Each method within these classes annotated with @Bean represents a bean definition. Spring's IoC container then uses these classes to create and manage your beans.

Let's start with a simple example. Suppose we have the same MessageService and MessageFormatter classes from our XML configuration example.

We can define these beans using Java configuration like this:

Java

```java
import org.springframework.context.annotation.Bean;

import org.springframework.context.annotation.Configuration;


@Configuration

public class AppConfig {


    @Bean

    public MessageFormatter messageFormatter() {

        return new MessageFormatter();

    }


    @Bean

    public MessageService
messageService(MessageFormatter formatter) {

        return new MessageService(formatter);

    }

}
```

In this code, we're using the @Configuration annotation to mark the AppConfig class as a configuration class. Inside this class, we have two methods, messageFormatter() and messageService(), both annotated with @Bean. These methods create and return instances of our beans. The messageService() method takes a MessageFormatter as an argument, which Spring automatically injects.

To load this configuration and use the beans, we'd write Java code like this:

```Java
import
org.springframework.context.ApplicationContext;

import
org.springframework.context.annotation.Annotation
ConfigApplicationContext;


public class Main {

    public static void main(String[] args) {

        ApplicationContext context = new
AnnotationConfigApplicationContext(AppConfig.clas
s);

        MessageService service =
context.getBean(MessageService.class);

        service.printMessage("Hello, Spring!");

    }

}
```

Here, we're using AnnotationConfigApplicationContext to load the AppConfig class. Then, we're using context.getBean(MessageService.class) to retrieve the messageService bean from the Spring container.

Now, let's look at a more complex example

Suppose we have the DatabaseService that depends on a DataSource and a TransactionManager. We can define these beans with properties and constructor arguments:

Java

```
import
org.springframework.context.annotation.Bean;

import
org.springframework.context.annotation.Configurat
ion;



@Configuration

public class DatabaseConfig {


    @Bean

    public MyDataSource dataSource() {

        MyDataSource dataSource = new
MyDataSource();


dataSource.setUrl("jdbc:mysql://localhost:3306/my
db");
```

```java
        dataSource.setUsername("user");

        dataSource.setPassword("password");

        return dataSource;

    }



    @Bean

    public MyTransactionManager
transactionManager() {

        return new MyTransactionManager();

    }



    @Bean

    public DatabaseService
databaseService(MyDataSource dataSource,
MyTransactionManager transactionManager) {

        return new DatabaseService(dataSource,
transactionManager);

    }

}
```

In this example, we're setting the properties of the MyDataSource bean directly in the dataSource() method. We're also passing the DataSource and TransactionManager beans as arguments to the databaseService() method.

A real-world example:

Consider a microservice architecture where each microservice has its own set of configurations. Using Java configuration, you can organize your beans and their dependencies in a modular and maintainable way. This makes it easier to manage and deploy your microservices.

Java configuration also supports features like bean scopes, initialization and destruction methods, and AOP aspects.

For instance, you can define a bean with a prototype scope:

```java
Java

import
org.springframework.context.annotation.Bean;

import
org.springframework.context.annotation.Configurat
ion;

import
org.springframework.context.annotation.Scope;


@Configuration

public class MyConfig {


    @Bean

    @Scope("prototype")

    public MyBean myBean() {
```

```java
        return new MyBean();

    }

}
```

Or define initialization and destruction methods:

```java
Java

import
org.springframework.context.annotation.Bean;

import
org.springframework.context.annotation.Configurat
ion;


@Configuration

public class MyConfig {


    @Bean(initMethod = "init", destroyMethod =
"destroy")

    public MyBean myBean() {

        return new MyBean();

    }

}
```

Java configuration is generally preferred over XML configuration because it's more concise, readable, and type-safe. It allows you to write your configuration code in Java, which makes it easier to refactor and maintain.

Here's an exercise:

Create a Spring application with two beans and wire them together using Java configuration. Experiment with different bean scopes and initialization/destruction methods. This will help you get comfortable with Java-based configuration and see how it works in practice.

3.3 Annotation-Based Configuration (@Component, etc.)

Alright, let's explore annotation-based configuration, which is the most concise and often the most convenient way to configure Spring applications. This approach leverages annotations to define beans and their dependencies directly within your classes, reducing the need for separate configuration files.

So, how does it work? You use annotations like @Component, @Service, @Repository, and @Controller to mark your classes as Spring beans. Then, you use annotations like @Autowired to inject dependencies. Spring's IoC container scans your classes for these annotations and automatically creates and wires the beans.

Let's start with a simple example

Suppose we have the MessageService and MessageFormatter classes again. We can define these beans using annotations like this:

Java

```
import org.springframework.stereotype.Component;
```

```java
@Component

class MessageFormatter {

    String format(String message) {

        return "Formatted: " + message;

    }

}



import
org.springframework.beans.factory.annotation.Auto
wired;

import org.springframework.stereotype.Component;



@Component

class MessageService {

    private final MessageFormatter formatter;


    @Autowired

    MessageService(MessageFormatter formatter) {

        this.formatter = formatter;

    }
```

```java
    void printMessage(String message) {

System.out.println(formatter.format(message));

    }

}
```

In this code, we're using the @Component annotation to mark both MessageFormatter and MessageService as Spring beans. The @Autowired annotation on the constructor of MessageService tells Spring to inject a MessageFormatter instance.

To enable annotation-based configuration, you need to tell Spring where to scan for these annotated classes.

You can do this using the @ComponentScan annotation in a @Configuration class:

```java
Java

import
org.springframework.context.annotation.ComponentS
can;

import
org.springframework.context.annotation.Configurat
ion;


@Configuration

@ComponentScan

public class AppConfig {

    // No explicit bean definitions needed!
```

}

By default, @ComponentScan scans the package of the @Configuration class.

You can also specify packages to scan:

Java

```
@ComponentScan("com.example.service")
```

To load this configuration and use the beans, you'd write Java code like this:

Java

```
import
org.springframework.context.ApplicationContext;

import
org.springframework.context.annotation.Annotation
ConfigApplicationContext;


public class Main {

    public static void main(String[] args) {

        ApplicationContext context = new
AnnotationConfigApplicationContext(AppConfig.clas
s);

        MessageService service =
context.getBean(MessageService.class);

        service.printMessage("Hello, Spring!");

    }
```

}

Notice how much simpler this is compared to XML or even Java configuration. We're not explicitly defining beans in a separate file; Spring handles it automatically.

Now, let's look at the other important annotations

- @Service: This is a specialization of @Component for service classes (classes that contain business logic). It's more of a semantic distinction, but it helps in code organization.
- @Repository: This is another specialization of @Component for data access classes (classes that interact with databases). It also provides some exception translation features.
- @Controller: This is a specialization of @Component for classes that handle web requests in Spring MVC.

Here's an example using @Service and @Repository:

Java

```java
import org.springframework.stereotype.Repository;


@Repository

class MyRepository {

    String getData() {

        return "Data from database";

    }

}
```

```java
import
org.springframework.beans.factory.annotation.Auto
wired;

import org.springframework.stereotype.Service;


@Service

class MyService {

    private final MyRepository repository;


    @Autowired

    MyService(MyRepository repository) {

        this.repository = repository;

    }


    String getDataFromDatabase() {

        return repository.getData();

    }

}
```

A real-world example:

In a complex application with many layers, annotation-based configuration allows you to define beans and their dependencies close to where they're used. This improves code readability and maintainability, especially when you're working with a large team.

Annotation-based configuration also supports features like bean scopes and lifecycle methods. You can use annotations like @Scope, @PostConstruct, and @PreDestroy to control these aspects.

Here's an exercise:

Create a Spring application with several beans using annotation-based configuration. Experiment with @Component, @Service, and @Repository. Also, try using @Scope to control the bean scopes. This will give you a good understanding of how annotation-based configuration works in practice.

Annotation-based configuration is a powerful and convenient way to configure Spring applications. It reduces boilerplate code and improves code organization, making your development process more efficient.

3.4 Externalizing Configuration with Properties

Alright, let's talk about externalizing configuration with properties files. This is a crucial technique for making your applications more flexible and adaptable to different environments. Instead of hardcoding values directly in your code, you can store them in external files and load them into your application. This allows you to change configuration settings without needing to recompile your code.

So, how does it work? You typically store your configuration settings in files with the .properties extension. These files contain key-value pairs, where the key represents the property name and the value represents the property value.

Here's a simple example of an application.properties file:

Properties

database.url=jdbc:mysql://localhost:3306/mydb

database.username=user

database.password=password

To load these properties into your Spring application, you can use the @PropertySource annotation in a @Configuration class. This annotation tells Spring to load the properties file from the specified location.

Here's an example:

```java
Java

import
org.springframework.context.annotation.Configurat
ion;

import
org.springframework.context.annotation.PropertySo
urce;


@Configuration

@PropertySource("classpath:application.properties
")

public class AppConfig {

    // ...

}
```

In[1] this code, we're using @PropertySource("classpath:application.properties") to tell Spring to load the application.properties file from the classpath.

Once you've loaded the properties, you can access them in your beans using the @Value annotation. This annotation injects the value of a property into a field or method parameter.

Here's an example:

```java
import
org.springframework.beans.factory.annotation.Valu
e;

import org.springframework.stereotype.Component;



@Component

class DatabaseConfig {


    @Value("${database.url}")

    private String url;


    @Value("${database.username}")

    private String username;


    @Value("${database.password}")
```

```
    private String password;


    void printDatabaseInfo() {

        System.out.println("URL: " + url);

        System.out.println("Username: " +
username);

        System.out.println("Password: " +
password);

    }

}
```

In this code, we're using @Value("${database.url}"),
@Value("${database.username}"), and
@Value("${database.password}") to inject the values of the
database.url, database.username, and database.password
properties into the url, username, and password fields,
respectively.

A real-world example:

Consider a web application that connects to a database. You might
want to externalize the database connection details (URL,
username, password) so you can easily change them when you
deploy the application to a different environment (e.g.,
development, testing, production). Using properties files, you can
store these details in an external file and load them into your
application.

You can also use placeholders in your properties files.

For example:

Properties

app.name=My Application

app.description=${app.name} - A great app

Spring will automatically resolve the ${app.name} placeholder.

Spring also supports different ways of specifying the location of your properties files. You can use classpath resources, file system resources, and even URLs.

Here's a practical exercise:

Create a Spring application that loads properties from a file. Define some properties like application name, version, and author. Then, inject these properties into a bean and print them to the console. Experiment with changing the values in the properties file and see how they're reflected in your application.

Externalizing configuration with properties files is a powerful technique that promotes flexibility and maintainability. It allows you to adapt your applications to different environments without modifying your code, making your deployment process much smoother.

3.5 Environment Profiles

Alright, let's discuss Spring's Environment Profiles. This feature is incredibly useful when you need to configure your application differently depending on the environment it's running in, such as development, testing, or production. It allows you to activate specific sets of beans and settings based on the active profile.

So, how do Environment Profiles work? You essentially define different configurations for different environments and then tell Spring which configuration to use at runtime. You do this using the @Profile annotation.

Here's a basic example

Let's say you have a DataSource bean, and you want to use an in-memory database for development and a real database for production. You can define two configuration classes, each annotated with @Profile:

```Java
import
org.springframework.context.annotation.Bean;

import
org.springframework.context.annotation.Configurat
ion;

import
org.springframework.context.annotation.Profile;


@Configuration

@Profile("dev")

public class DevConfig {


    @Bean

    public DataSource dataSource() {

        // Configuration for in-memory database
```

```
        return new InMemoryDataSource();

    }

}


@Configuration

@Profile("prod")

public class ProdConfig {


    @Bean

    public DataSource dataSource() {

        // Configuration for production database

        return new ProductionDataSource();

    }

}
```

In this code, @Profile("dev") indicates that DevConfig should be used when the "dev" profile is active, and @Profile("prod") indicates that ProdConfig should be used when the "prod" profile is active.

To tell Spring which profile to activate, you can use the spring.profiles.active property.

You can set this property in various ways, such as:

- System property: -Dspring.profiles.active=dev
- Environment variable: SPRING_PROFILES_ACTIVE=dev

- Web application context parameter: In web.xml for traditional web applications.
- Spring Boot's application.properties or application.yml: spring.profiles.active=dev

If you're using Spring Boot, the application.properties (or application.yml) file is a common place to set this property.

You can also activate multiple profiles at once by separating them with commas:

spring.profiles.active=dev,h2

This can be useful if you have a base set of configurations and then add environment-specific configurations.

Here's a more complete example

Let's say you have a logging service, and you want to use a simple console logger for development and a more robust file logger for production:

```Java
import
org.springframework.context.annotation.Bean;

import
org.springframework.context.annotation.Configurat
ion;

import
org.springframework.context.annotation.Profile;


interface Logger {
```

```java
    void log(String message);

}


@Configuration

@Profile("dev")

public class DevLoggingConfig {


    @Bean

    public Logger logger() {

        return new ConsoleLogger();

    }

}


@Configuration

@Profile("prod")

public class ProdLoggingConfig {


    @Bean

    public Logger logger() {

        return new FileLogger();
```

```java
    }

}


class ConsoleLogger implements Logger {

    public void log(String message) {

        System.out.println("DEV LOG: " +
message);

    }

}


class FileLogger implements Logger {

    public void log(String message) {

        // Implementation to write to a file

        System.out.println("PROD LOG: " +
message);

    }

}
```

A real-world example:

In a microservices architecture, you might have different configurations for each microservice based on its environment. For example, the service responsible for handling payments might have different security settings in development and production.

Environment Profiles allow you to manage these configurations effectively.

Here's a practical exercise:

Create a Spring application with two profiles: "dev" and "prod". Define a simple bean (e.g., a message provider) and provide different implementations for each profile. Then, use Spring Boot's application.properties to switch between the profiles and observe the behavior of your application.

Environment Profiles are a powerful tool for managing environment-specific configurations in your Spring applications. They help you keep your configuration clean, organized, and adaptable to different deployment scenarios.

Chapter 4: Spring AOP (Aspect-Oriented Programming)

So, what's AOP all about? It's a programming paradigm that aims to increase modularity by allowing the separation of cross-cutting concerns. Now, that might sound a bit technical, so let's break it down.

4.1 Understanding AOP and Cross-Cutting Concerns

Okay, let's really get into the core of AOP and cross-cutting concerns. This is a topic that, once you grasp it, will significantly change how you think about designing your applications.

So, AOP, or Aspect-Oriented Programming, is a paradigm that allows us to structure our code in a way that separates concerns. Now, what does that mean? To understand AOP, we first need to understand what "concerns" are in programming.

In object-oriented programming (OOP), we typically organize our code into classes and objects. Each class is responsible for a specific function or responsibility. For example, you might have a class for handling user authentication, another for processing orders, and so on. This works great for the core business logic of your application.

However, some functionalities don't fit neatly into this class-based structure. These are the "cross-cutting concerns." They are functionalities that affect multiple parts of your application. Think of them as threads that weave through different classes and methods.

Let's look at some common examples:

- Logging: In a real-world application, you often need to log information about what's happening. You might want to log when a user logs in, when an order is placed, or when an exception occurs. You could put logging code in every method that needs it, but that leads to a lot of duplication.
- Security: Similarly, you might need to enforce security rules, such as authentication and authorization, across various parts of your application. You wouldn't want to repeat the same security checks in every method.
- Transaction Management: If you're working with databases, you often need to manage transactions. You might want to start a transaction before a series of database operations and commit it if everything succeeds or roll it back if something goes wrong. Again, you don't want to duplicate this transaction management code in every method that interacts with the database.

The problem with these cross-cutting concerns is that they "cut across" the boundaries of your classes. If yo

u implement them in a traditional way, you end up with "tangled" code. Your business logic classes become cluttered with logging, security, or transaction management code.

This makes your code:

- Harder to read: It's difficult to see the core business logic when it's mixed with other code.
- Harder to maintain: If you need to change the logging mechanism, you have to change it in every class.
- Harder to test: It's difficult to test the business logic in isolation when it's tightly coupled with cross-cutting concerns.

AOP provides a solution to this problem. It allows you to separate these cross-cutting concerns into separate modules called "aspects." An aspect is like a self-contained unit that encapsulates a specific cross-cutting concern.

Here's a simple analogy: think of a play. The actors are like your objects, and they focus on their roles. But there are also stagehands who handle things like lighting, sound, and scenery. These are like aspects; they handle the cross-cutting concerns without cluttering the actors' performances.

With AOP, you define your core business logic in your classes, and you define the cross-cutting concerns in aspects. Then, you use AOP to "weave" the aspects into your classes at specific points. This results in cleaner, more modular, and more maintainable code.

Let's illustrate this with a simple example.Suppose you have a service class that performs some business logic:

```Java
class MyService {

    void doSomething() {

        System.out.println("Performing business logic");

    }

}
```

Now, let's say you want to add logging to this method.

Without AOP, you might modify the doSomething() method:

Java

```java
class MyService {

    void doSomething() {

        System.out.println("Logging: Before doing something");

        System.out.println("Performing business logic");

        System.out.println("Logging: After doing something");

    }

}
```

This works, but it clutters the doSomething() method with logging code. With AOP, you could define a separate logging aspect and apply it to the doSomething() method. This keeps the MyService class clean and focused on its core responsibility.

Here's a practical exercise:

Think about a project you've worked on. Identify some cross-cutting concerns that were present in the code. How was this code implemented? Could AOP have been used to improve the design?

Okay, I understand. I will adhere to the prompt and always start directly with the main heading.

4.2 Defining Aspects, Advice, and Pointcuts

Okay, let's break down the core components of AOP: aspects, advice, and pointcuts. These are the building blocks that allow you to implement cross-cutting concerns effectively.

So, we established that AOP helps us separate cross-cutting concerns into modules. These modules are called **aspects**. Think of an aspect as a class that encapsulates a specific piece of functionality that you want to apply to multiple parts of your application. For example, you might have a LoggingAspect that handles logging, a SecurityAspect that handles authorization, or a TransactionAspect that handles transaction management.

Now, within an aspect, you define what action to take and when to take it. The action is called advice, and the "when" is defined by a pointcut.

Advice

Advice is the actual code that gets executed by the aspect. It's the "what" part of AOP. Spring AOP defines several types of advice, each corresponding to a different point in the execution of a method.

- Before advice: This advice runs before the execution of a method. You can use it for things like authentication, authorization, or input validation.

```Java

import org.aspectj.lang.JoinPoint;

import org.aspectj.lang.annotation.Aspect;
```

```java
import org.aspectj.lang.annotation.Before;

import org.springframework.stereotype.Component;


@Aspect

@Component

class MyAspect {


    @Before("execution(*
com.example.service.*.*(..))")

    public void beforeAdvice(JoinPoint joinPoint)
{

        String methodName =
joinPoint.getSignature().getName();

        System.out.println("Before executing: " +
methodName);

    }

}
```

In this[1] example, @Before annotates the beforeAdvice method, indicating that it should run before the execution of any method matching the pointcut "execution(* com.example.service.*.*(..))". The JoinPoint object provides access to information about the method being called, such as its name and arguments.

- After returning advice: This advice runs after the execution of a method *if* the method completes successfully (i.e., without throwing an exception). You can use it to log the return value or perform some cleanup.

Java

```java
import org.aspectj.lang.JoinPoint;

import org.aspectj.lang.annotation.AfterReturning;

import org.aspectj.lang.annotation.Aspect;

import org.springframework.stereotype.Component;


@Aspect

@Component

class MyAspect {


    @AfterReturning(pointcut = "execution(* com.example.service.*.*(..))", returning = "result")

    public void afterReturningAdvice(JoinPoint joinPoint, Object result) {

        String methodName = joinPoint.getSignature().getName();
```

```
    System.out.println("After returning from:
" + methodName + ", result: " + result);

    }

}
```

Here, @AfterReturning is used, and the returning attribute specifies the name of the parameter that will hold the return value of the method.

- After throwing advice: This advice runs after the execution of a method *if* the method throws an exception. You can use it to handle exceptions, log errors, or perform rollback operations.

Java

```
import org.aspectj.lang.JoinPoint;

import org.aspectj.lang.annotation.AfterThrowing;

import org.aspectj.lang.annotation.Aspect;

import org.springframework.stereotype.Component;


@Aspect

@Component

class MyAspect {
```

```java
    @AfterThrowing(pointcut = "execution(*
com.example.service.*.*(..))", throwing = "ex")

    public void afterThrowingAdvice(JoinPoint
joinPoint, Throwable ex) {

        String methodName =
joinPoint.getSignature().getName();

        System.out.println("After throwing from:
" + methodName + ", exception: " + ex);

    }

}
```

@AfterThrowing is used, and the throwing attribute specifies the name of the parameter that will hold the exception thrown by the method.

- After (finally) advice: This advice runs after the execution of a method, regardless of whether the method completes successfully or throws an exception. It's similar to the finally block in a try-catch statement. You can use it for cleanup operations that must always be performed.

Java

```java
import org.aspectj.lang.JoinPoint;

import org.aspectj.lang.annotation.After;

import org.aspectj.lang.annotation.Aspect;

import org.springframework.stereotype.Component;
```

```java
@Aspect

@Component

class MyAspect {


    @After("execution(*
com.example.service.*.*(..))")

    public void afterAdvice(JoinPoint joinPoint)
{

        String methodName =
joinPoint.getSignature().getName();

        System.out.println("After (finally)
executing: " + methodName);

    }

}
```

@After is used to specify advice that always runs.

- Around advice: This is the most powerful type of advice. It surrounds the execution of a method, giving you complete control before and after the method call. You can even choose to proceed with the method call or not.

import org.aspectj.lang.ProceedingJoinPoint;

import org.aspectj.lang.annotation.Around;

import org.aspectj.lang.annotation.Aspect;2

```java
import org.springframework.stereotype.Component;

@Aspect
@Component
class MyAspect {


    @Around("execution(* com.example.service.*.*(..))")

    public Object aroundAdvice(ProceedingJoinPoint proceedingJoinPoint) throws Throwable {

        String methodName = proceedingJoinPoint.getSignature().getName();

        System.out.println("Around: Before executing: " + methodName);

        Object result = proceedingJoinPoint.proceed(); // Execute the method

        System.out.println("Around: After executing: " + methodName + ", result: " + result);

        return result;

    }

}
```

`@Around` advice receives a `ProceedingJoinPoint`, which allows it to control whether the original method execution proceeds. It's crucial for tasks like transaction management or security checks.

Pointcuts

Now, the "when" part. A pointcut is a predicate that matches join points. A join point is a specific point in the execution of your application where an aspect can be applied. Common join points include method calls, method executions, constructor calls, and exception handling.

You define pointcuts using expressions. Spring AOP uses AspectJ pointcut expressions, which are quite powerful.

Here are some examples:

- execution(* com.example.service.*.*(..)): This pointcut matches the execution of any method in any class in the com.example.service package. The * wildcard matches any return type, any class name, any method name, and .. matches any number of arguments.
- within(com.example.dao.*): This pointcut matches any join point within classes in the com.example.dao package.
- @annotation(com.example.annotation.Loggable): This pointcut matches any join point where the executed method is annotated with the @Loggable annotation.

Putting It All Together

So, to define an aspect, you create a class, annotate it with @Aspect and @Component (to make it a Spring bean), and then define your advice methods. In each advice method, you specify the pointcut using the appropriate annotation (@Before, @AfterReturning, etc.).

Here's a practical exercise:

Think of a simple application (e.g., a calculator). Identify a cross-cutting concern (e.g., logging). Define an aspect to handle this concern, using different types of advice and pointcut expressions. This will help you solidify your understanding of these core AOP concepts. For example, you could log every addition and subtraction operation, including the arguments and the result. This exercise will show you how to apply AOP to a real, albeit simple, problem.

4.3 Implementing Logging with AOP

Okay, let's put AOP into action and see how we can use it to implement logging. Logging is a classic example of a cross-cutting concern, and AOP provides an elegant way to handle it.

So, why is logging a cross-cutting concern? Because you often need to log information in various parts of your application: when a method is called, when a method returns, when an exception is thrown, and so on. If you implement logging directly in your business logic classes, you'll end up with a lot of duplicated code, making your classes harder to read and maintain.

AOP allows you to separate the logging logic into a separate aspect and apply it to the appropriate methods using pointcuts. This keeps your business logic clean and focused.

Let's start with a simple example. Suppose we have a service class with a few methods:

Java

```
import org.springframework.stereotype.Service;
```

```java
@Service

class MyService {


    void doSomething() {

        System.out.println("Doing something");

    }


    String getData(int id) {

        System.out.println("Getting data for id:
" + id);

        return "Data for id: " + id;

    }


    void processData(String data) {

        System.out.println("Processing data: " +
data);

    }

}
```

Now, let's say we want to log the following information for each method call:

- The method name
- The method arguments
- The method's return value (if any)

We can create a LoggingAspect to handle this.

Here's how it might look:

```java
Java

import org.aspectj.lang.JoinPoint;

import org.aspectj.lang.ProceedingJoinPoint;

import
org.aspectj.lang.annotation.AfterReturning;

import org.aspectj.lang.annotation.Around;

import org.aspectj.lang.annotation.Aspect;

import org.aspectj.lang.annotation.Before;

import org.springframework.stereotype.Component;

import java.util.Arrays;


@Aspect

@Component

class LoggingAspect {


    @Before("execution(*
com.example.service.*.*(..))")

    public void logMethodCall(JoinPoint
joinPoint) {
```

```java
        String methodName =
joinPoint.getSignature().getName();

        Object[] args = joinPoint.getArgs();

        System.out.println("Before " + methodName
+ " with args: " + Arrays.toString(args));

    }



    @AfterReturning(pointcut = "execution(*
com.example.service.*.*(..))", returning =
"result")
    public void logMethodReturnValue(JoinPoint
joinPoint, Object result) {

        String methodName =
joinPoint.getSignature().getName();

        System.out.println("After " + methodName
+ " returns: " + result);

    }



    @Around("execution(*
com.example.service.*.*(..))")
    public Object
logExecutionTime(ProceedingJoinPoint joinPoint)
throws Throwable {

        long start = System.currentTimeMillis();

        Object proceed = joinPoint.proceed();
```

```
        long executionTime =
System.currentTimeMillis() - start;


System.out.println(joinPoint.getSignature() + "
executed in " + executionTime + "ms");

        return proceed;

    }

}
```

Let's break down this aspect:

- @Aspect and @Component: These annotations mark this class as an aspect and a Spring bean, respectively.
- @Before("execution(* com.example.service.*.*(..))"): This @Before advice runs before any method in any class in the com.example.service package. It logs the method name and its arguments.
- @AfterReturning(pointcut = "execution(* com.example.service.*.*(..))", returning = "result"): This @AfterReturning advice runs after a method in the com.example.service package returns successfully. It logs the method name and the return value. The returning attribute specifies the name of the parameter (result) that will hold the return value.
- @Around("execution(* com.example.service.*.*(..))"): This @Around advice measures the execution time of a method. It logs the method signature and the execution time. @Around advice has the ability to control the execution of the method, which is why it's used for this purpose.

To enable AOP in your Spring application, you can use the @EnableAspectJAutoProxy annotation in a @Configuration class:

```Java
import
org.springframework.context.annotation.Configurat
ion;

import
org.springframework.context.annotation.EnableAspe
ctJAutoProxy;


@Configuration

@EnableAspectJAutoProxy

public class AppConfig {

    // Other configurations

}
```

Now, when you run your application, you'll see logging information printed to the console for each method call.

A real-world example:

Consider a complex enterprise application with many layers and modules. Logging is crucial for debugging, monitoring, and auditing. Using AOP, you can implement a centralized logging aspect that handles logging consistently across the entire application, without cluttering your business logic classes.

Here's a practical exercise:

1. Create a simple Spring application with a few service classes.
2. Define a logging aspect that logs method calls, arguments, and return values.

3. Use different types of advice (@Before, @AfterReturning, @Around) to implement the logging logic.
4. Experiment with different pointcut expressions to apply the logging aspect to specific methods or classes.

This exercise will help you solidify your understanding of how to use AOP to implement logging and see the benefits of separating cross-cutting concerns.

4.4 Implementing Security with AOP

Okay, let's explore how AOP can be used to implement security in your applications. Security, like logging, is a cross-cutting concern that often needs to be applied to multiple parts of your code. AOP provides a clean way to separate security logic from your core business logic.

So, what kind of security concerns can AOP address? We'll focus on authentication and authorization.

- Authentication: Verifying the identity of a user.
- Authorization: Determining what resources a user is allowed to access.

Without AOP, you might end up with security checks scattered throughout your methods, leading to code duplication and making it difficult to maintain and update your security policies.

AOP allows you to encapsulate this security logic in aspects and apply it to specific methods using pointcuts.

Let's start with a basic example

Suppose we have a service with methods that should only be accessible to users with a specific role:

Java

```java
import org.springframework.stereotype.Service;


@Service

class MyService {


    void adminMethod() {

        System.out.println("Admin method
called");

    }


    void userMethod() {

        System.out.println("User method called");

    }


    void publicMethod() {

        System.out.println("Public method
called");

    }

}
```

We can create a SecurityAspect to enforce authorization.

Here's a simplified example:

```Java
import org.aspectj.lang.ProceedingJoinPoint;

import org.aspectj.lang.annotation.Around;

import org.aspectj.lang.annotation.Aspect;

import org.springframework.stereotype.Component;


@Aspect

@Component

class SecurityAspect {


    @Around("@annotation(AdminOnly)")

    public Object
checkAdminAccess(ProceedingJoinPoint joinPoint)
throws Throwable {

        if (currentUserHasRole("ADMIN")) {

            return joinPoint.proceed(); //
Proceed with the method call

        } else {

            throw new SecurityException("Access
denied: Admin role required");
```

```java
        }

    }


    @Around("@annotation(UserOrAdmin)")

    public Object
checkUserOrAdminAccess(ProceedingJoinPoint
joinPoint) throws Throwable {

        if (currentUserHasRole("USER") ||
currentUserHasRole("ADMIN")) {

            return joinPoint.proceed();

        } else {

            throw new SecurityException("Access
denied: User or Admin role required");

        }

    }


    private boolean currentUserHasRole(String
role) {

        // In a real application, you'd get the
current user's roles from

        // the security context (e.g., Spring
Security's SecurityContextHolder)

        // For simplicity, we'll simulate it
here.
```

```java
        if (role.equals("ADMIN")) {

            return Math.random() < 0.5; //
Simulate random admin access

        } else if (role.equals("USER")) {

            return true; // Simulate always
having user access

        }

        return false;

    }

}


import java.lang.annotation.ElementType;

import java.lang.annotation.Retention;

import java.lang.annotation.RetentionPolicy;

import java.lang.annotation.Target;


@Retention(RetentionPolicy.RUNTIME)

@Target(ElementType.METHOD)

public @interface AdminOnly {

}
```

```java
import java.lang.annotation.ElementType;

import java.lang.annotation.Retention;

import java.lang.annotation.RetentionPolicy;

import java.lang.annotation.Target;


@Retention(RetentionPolicy.RUNTIME)

@Target(ElementType.METHOD)

public @interface UserOrAdmin {

}
```

Let's break down this aspect:

- @Aspect and @Component: These annotations mark this class as an aspect and a Spring bean.
- @Around("@annotation(AdminOnly)"): This @Around advice applies to methods annotated with the @AdminOnly annotation. It checks if the current user has the "ADMIN" role. If so, it proceeds with the method call; otherwise, it throws a SecurityException.
- @Around("@annotation(UserOrAdmin)"): This @Around advice applies to methods annotated with the @UserOrAdmin annotation. It checks if the current user has either the "USER" or "ADMIN" role.
- currentUserHasRole(String role): This method simulates checking the current user's roles. In a real application, you would typically use a security framework like Spring Security to manage authentication and authorization. You would retrieve the user's roles from the SecurityContextHolder.

- @Retention(RetentionPolicy.RUNTIME) and @Target(ElementType.METHOD): These annotations define custom annotations (@AdminOnly and @UserOrAdmin) that can be used to mark methods for security checks. @Retention(RetentionPolicy.RUNTIME) ensures that the annotations are available at runtime, which is necessary for AOP to work. @Target(ElementType.METHOD) specifies that the annotations can only be applied to methods.

To use this aspect, you would annotate your service methods:

Java

```java
import org.springframework.stereotype.Service;


@Service

class MyService {


    @AdminOnly

    void adminMethod() {

        System.out.println("Admin method called");

    }


    @UserOrAdmin
```

```java
void userMethod() {

    System.out.println("User method called");

}



void publicMethod() {

    System.out.println("Public method
called");

}

}
```

Now, when you call adminMethod(), the SecurityAspect will check if the current user has the "ADMIN" role. If not, a SecurityException will be thrown.

A real-world example:

Consider an e-commerce application. You might have methods for managing products that should only be accessible to administrators, methods for placing orders that should only be accessible to logged-in users, and methods for browsing products that should be accessible to everyone. AOP allows you to implement these security rules in a centralized and maintainable way.

Here's a practical exercise:

1. Create a simple Spring application with a few service methods.
2. Define custom annotations to represent different roles or permissions.

3. Implement a security aspect that checks the current user's roles before allowing access to methods annotated with these custom annotations.
4. Simulate user authentication and authorization (for simplicity). In a real application, you would integrate with a security framework like Spring Security.

This exercise will help you understand how to use AOP to implement security and see the benefits of separating security logic from your business logic.

4.5 Implementing Transaction Management with AOP

Okay, let's discuss how AOP can be used to handle transaction management in your Spring applications. Transaction management is crucial for ensuring data consistency and integrity, especially when dealing with databases. It's another excellent example of a cross-cutting concern that AOP can address effectively.

So, what is transaction management? In simple terms, a transaction is a sequence of operations that should be treated as a single unit of work. Either all operations in the transaction succeed, or none of them do.

This is often referred to as the ACID properties:

- Atomicity: The entire transaction is treated as a single unit. Either all changes are applied, or none are.
- Consistency: The transaction moves the system from one valid state to another.
- Isolation: Transactions are isolated from each other, preventing interference.
- Durability: Once a transaction is committed, the changes are permanent.

Without proper transaction management, you can end up with inconsistent data. For example, if you're transferring funds between accounts, you wouldn't want the money to be deducted from one account but not credited to the other.

Spring provides declarative transaction management, which means you can define transaction boundaries using configuration (often with AOP) instead of writing explicit transaction management code in your business logic. This makes your code cleaner and more maintainable.

Let's illustrate this with an example

Suppose we have a service that performs a series of database operations:

Java

```java
import org.springframework.stereotype.Service;



@Service

class MyService {



    void operation1() {

        System.out.println("Performing operation 1");

        // Database operation 1

    }
```

```java
    void operation2() {

        System.out.println("Performing operation
2");

        // Database operation 2

    }


    void operation3() {

        System.out.println("Performing operation
3");

        // Database operation 3

    }

}
```

We want to ensure that these operations are executed within a single transaction. If any operation fails, all previous operations should be rolled back.

Here's how we can use AOP to achieve this:

```java
Java

import org.aspectj.lang.ProceedingJoinPoint;

import org.aspectj.lang.annotation.Around;

import org.aspectj.lang.annotation.Aspect;

import org.springframework.stereotype.Component;
```

```java
import
org.springframework.transaction.PlatformTransacti
onManager;

import
org.springframework.transaction.TransactionStatus
;

import
org.springframework.transaction.support.DefaultTr
ansactionDefinition;


@Aspect

@Component

class TransactionAspect {


    private final PlatformTransactionManager
transactionManager;


    public
TransactionAspect(PlatformTransactionManager
transactionManager) {

        this.transactionManager =
transactionManager;

    }
```

```
    @Around("execution(*
com.example.service.*.*(..))")

    public Object
manageTransaction(ProceedingJoinPoint joinPoint)
throws Throwable {

        TransactionStatus status =
transactionManager.getTransaction(new
DefaultTransactionDefinition());

        try {

            Object result = joinPoint.proceed();
// Execute the method

            transactionManager.commit(status); //
Commit the transaction

            return result;

        } catch (Throwable e) {

            transactionManager.rollback(status);
// Rollback the transaction

            throw e;

        }

    }

}
```

Let's break down this aspect:

- @Aspect and @Component: These annotations mark this
  class as an aspect and a Spring bean.

- PlatformTransactionManager: This is Spring's interface for transaction management. You need to inject an implementation of this interface (e.g., DataSourceTransactionManager for JDBC).
- @Around("execution(* com.example.service.*.*(..))"): This @Around advice applies to any method in any class in the com.example.service package. This is a broad pointcut and you'll often want to refine it.
- transactionManager.getTransaction(new DefaultTransactionDefinition()): This line starts a new transaction.
- joinPoint.proceed(): This executes the method being advised.
- transactionManager.commit(status): This commits the transaction if the method executes successfully.
- transactionManager.rollback(status): This rolls back the transaction if the method throws an exception.

To enable Spring's declarative transaction management with AOP, you typically use the @EnableTransactionManagement annotation in a @Configuration class:

```java
Java

import
org.springframework.context.annotation.Configurat
ion;

import
org.springframework.transaction.annotation.Enable
TransactionManagement;


@Configuration

@EnableTransactionManagement
```

```
public class AppConfig {

    // Other configurations

}
```

Now, when any method in MyService is called, the TransactionAspect will automatically manage the transaction.

A real-world example:

Consider an online banking application. When a user transfers funds, several database operations might be involved: deducting the amount from the sender's account, adding the amount to the recipient's account, and updating transaction logs. It's crucial that these operations are performed atomically. If any operation fails, the entire transaction should be rolled back to maintain data consistency. AOP simplifies managing such transactions.

Here's a practical exercise:

1. Create a simple Spring application that interacts with a database.
2. Implement a service with methods that perform multiple database operations.
3. Configure a DataSourceTransactionManager and inject it into your transaction aspect.
4. Define a transaction aspect that manages transactions around your service methods.
5. Simulate a failure during one of the database operations and verify that the entire transaction is rolled back.

This exercise will help you understand how to use AOP to implement transaction management and appreciate the benefits of declarative transaction management in Spring.

Chapter 5: Spring MVC (Model-View-Controller)

So, you want to build web applications with Spring? That's where Spring MVC comes in. It's a framework that helps you structure your web applications in a clean and organized way, following the Model-View-Controller pattern.

5.1 Building Web Applications with Spring MVC

Okay, let's talk about building web applications with Spring MVC. This is a big topic, but we'll break it down step by step so you get a clear understanding.

Spring MVC is Spring's module for building web applications. It's built on the Model-View-Controller (MVC) design pattern, which is a fundamental concept in web development. To really grasp Spring MVC, we need to first understand what MVC is and why it's so important.

The Model-View-Controller (MVC) Pattern

MVC is an architectural pattern that separates an application into three interconnected parts:

- **Model**: This represents the data of your application. It's where you store and manage the information. Think of it as the data structures and logic that manipulate that data. For example, in an e-commerce application, the model would include objects representing products, customers, orders, and the methods to retrieve, create, update, and delete them. It's not just the database; it's the objects and code that interact with the database and any other data sources.

- **View**: This is what the user sees. It's the user interface of your application. The view is responsible for displaying the data from the model to the user in a presentable format (e.g., HTML, CSS). It focuses on presentation and should ideally contain minimal application logic. Spring MVC supports various view technologies, which we'll discuss later.
- **Controller:** This acts as the intermediary between the model and the view. It handles user input, interacts with the model to retrieve or update data, and then selects the appropriate view to display the results. The controller receives the request, processes it, and orchestrates the interaction between the model and the view.

Why Use MVC?

MVC provides several benefits:

- Separation of Concerns: It clearly separates the different parts of the application, making it easier to develop, test, and maintain. This is crucial for large applications with complex functionality. Developers can specialize in specific areas (e.g., UI design, data access) without needing to understand the entire codebase.
- Modularity: It promotes modularity, as each component has a specific responsibility. This makes the application more flexible and reusable. You can swap out different views without changing the controller, or you can reuse the model in different applications.
- Testability: It improves testability, as each component can be tested in isolation. You can write unit tests for your controllers and model classes without needing to render the view. This makes your tests more focused and reliable.
- Maintainability: It enhances maintainability, as changes in one component are less likely to affect other components. If you need to change the look and feel of your application,

you can modify the view without touching the controller or model.

How Spring MVC Implements MVC

Spring MVC provides a framework for implementing the MVC pattern in Java web applications.

Let's see how it works:

1. The DispatcherServlet: This is the heart of Spring MVC. It's the front controller that handles all incoming HTTP requests. When a user sends a request to your application, the DispatcherServlet receives it. You need to configure this servlet in your web application's configuration file (usually web.xml for traditional web applications). However, if you're using Spring Boot, this is typically handled automatically through auto-configuration, simplifying the setup.

2. HandlerMapping: Once the DispatcherServlet receives a request, it needs to figure out which controller should handle it. That's where HandlerMapping comes in. It determines the appropriate controller based on the request's URL, HTTP method (GET, POST, etc.), and other criteria. Spring MVC provides several built-in HandlerMapping implementations, such as RequestMappingHandlerMapping (which is commonly used with annotations like @RequestMapping). You can also create your own if you have very specific needs, but the built-in ones are usually sufficient.

3. Controller: The controller is where you write your application logic. It receives the request, processes it (which might involve interacting with the model to retrieve or update data), and then prepares the data for the view. In Spring MVC, controllers are typically Java classes annotated with @Controller. They act as coordinators, orchestrating the interaction between the model and the view.

4. ModelAndView: Controllers don't directly render the view. Instead, they typically return a ModelAndView object (though there are other options). This object holds both the data that needs to be displayed (the model) and the name of the view that should be used to render it. The model is usually a Map that contains key-value pairs representing the data.

5. ViewResolver: The DispatcherServlet uses a ViewResolver to determine the actual View object based on the view name returned by the controller. Spring MVC supports various view technologies, such as JSP (JavaServer Pages), Thymeleaf, and others. The ViewResolver selects the appropriate view implementation. For example, ThymeleafViewResolver is used to resolve Thymeleaf views.

6. View: The View is responsible for rendering the output to the user. It takes the data provided by the controller (through the ModelAndView) and formats it into the desired output format (usually HTML). The view uses a template engine (like Thymeleaf or JSP) to dynamically generate the HTML, embedding the data from the model.

A Simple Example

Let's illustrate this with a very basic example. Suppose you want to create a web page that displays a greeting message.

1. We'd have a controller that handles the request and prepares the greeting message.
2. We'd have a view (e.g., an HTML page using Thymeleaf) that displays the message.

Here's a simplified code snippet (using Spring Boot, which simplifies setup):

Java

```java
import org.springframework.stereotype.Controller;

import org.springframework.ui.Model;

import org.springframework.web.bind.annotation.GetMapping;


@Controller

public class GreetingController {


    @GetMapping("/greeting")

    public String greeting(Model model) {

        model.addAttribute("message", "Hello, Spring MVC!");

        return "greeting"; // The name of the view (e.g., greeting.html)

    }

}
```

In this example:

- @Controller marks GreetingController as a controller. This tells Spring MVC that this class is responsible for handling web requests.
- @GetMapping("/greeting") maps requests to the /greeting URL to the greeting() method. This annotation is a shorthand for @RequestMapping(value = "/greeting",

method = RequestMethod.GET) and makes the code more concise.

- The greeting() method takes a Model object as a parameter. Spring MVC provides this object, and you use it to add data that will be passed to the view. In this case, we're adding a key-value pair where the key is "message" and the value is "Hello, Spring MVC!".
- The greeting() method returns the name of the view ("greeting"). Spring MVC will use a ViewResolver to find the appropriate view (e.g., a Thymeleaf template named greeting.html).

And here's a simple Thymeleaf view (greeting.html):

HTML

```
<!DOCTYPE HTML>

<html xmlns:th="http://www.thymeleaf.org">



<head>

    <title>Greeting</title>

</head>



<body>

    <h1>Greeting Page</h1>

    <p th:text="${message}"></p>

</body>
```

```
</html>
```

This view displays the message passed from the controller.

- th:text="${message}" is a Thymeleaf expression that accesses the "message" attribute from the model and displays its value within the <p> tag.

A real-world example:

Consider a content management system (CMS). The model would include articles, users, and categories. The view would display the articles in different formats (e.g., a list, a detailed view). The controller would handle user actions like creating a new article, editing an existing one, or searching for articles.

Spring MVC simplifies the process of building web applications by providing a robust and flexible framework for implementing the MVC pattern. It handles the underlying mechanics of web requests and responses, allowing you to focus on the core logic of your application.

Here's a practical exercise:

Create a simple Spring MVC application that displays a list of products. Allow the user to view the details of a specific product. This exercise will help you understand how to pass data between the controller and the view and how to handle different types of requests. You can expand on this by adding functionality to add or edit products, further solidifying your knowledge.

5.2 Handling HTTP Requests and Responses

Okay, let's talk about how Spring MVC handles HTTP requests and responses. This is the core of how web applications communicate, so understanding it is fundamental.

In web development, HTTP (Hypertext Transfer Protocol) is the protocol used for communication between web browsers and web servers. When a user interacts with a web page (e.g., clicks a link, submits a form), the browser sends an HTTP request to the server. The server processes the request and sends back an HTTP response.[1] Spring MVC provides powerful mechanisms to handle these requests and construct appropriate responses.

Mapping Requests to Controllers

The first step in handling a request is to determine which controller should process it. Spring MVC uses annotations to map HTTP requests to controller methods.

- @RequestMapping: This is the most versatile annotation for mapping requests. You can use it to map requests based on various criteria:
    - URL path: Specifies the URL pattern that the method should handle.
    - HTTP method: Specifies the HTTP method (GET, POST, PUT, DELETE, etc.) that the method should handle.
    - Request parameters: Specifies that the method should handle requests with certain request parameters.
    - Request headers: Specifies that the method should handle requests with certain request headers.

- Media types: Specifies that the method should handle requests with certain media types (e.g., "application/json", "text/html").

Here's an example:

```
Java
```

```java
import org.springframework.stereotype.Controller;

import org.springframework.web.bind.annotation.RequestMapping;

import org.springframework.web.bind.annotation.RequestMethod;

import org.springframework.web.bind.annotation.RequestParam;

import org.springframework.web.servlet.ModelAndView;


@Controller

public class MyController {


    @RequestMapping(value = "/greet", method = RequestMethod.GET)
```

```java
    public ModelAndView
greet(@RequestParam("name") String name) {

        ModelAndView modelAndView = new
ModelAndView("greeting");

        modelAndView.addObject("greetingMessage",
"Hello, " + name + "!");

        return modelAndView;

    }



    @RequestMapping(value = "/submit", method =
RequestMethod.POST)

    public String
submitForm(@RequestParam("data") String formData)
{

        // Process the form data

        System.out.println("Received data: " +
formData);

        return "formSuccess"; // View name

    }

}
```

In this example:

o   @Controller marks the class as a controller.

- - @RequestMapping(value = "/greet", method = RequestMethod.GET) maps GET requests to the /greet URL to the greet() method.
  - @RequestParam("name") String name retrieves the value of the "name" request parameter.
  - @RequestMapping(value = "/submit", method = RequestMethod.POST) maps POST requests to the /submit URL to the submitForm() method.
- Shorthand Annotations: To simplify common scenarios, Spring MVC provides shorthand annotations for specific HTTP methods:
  - @GetMapping: Maps GET requests.
  - @PostMapping: Maps POST requests.
  - @PutMapping: Maps PUT requests (used for updating resources).
  - @DeleteMapping: Maps DELETE requests (used for deleting resources).

Here's the previous example using shorthand annotations:

Java

```java
import org.springframework.stereotype.Controller;

import org.springframework.web.bind.annotation.GetMapping;

import org.springframework.web.bind.annotation.PostMapping;
```

```java
import
org.springframework.web.bind.annotation.RequestPa
ram;

import
org.springframework.web.servlet.ModelAndView;


@Controller
public class MyController {


    @GetMapping("/greet")
    public ModelAndView
greet(@RequestParam("name") String name) {

        ModelAndView modelAndView = new
ModelAndView("greeting");

        modelAndView.addObject("greetingMessage",
"Hello, " + name + "!");

        return modelAndView;

    }


    @PostMapping("/submit")

    pub
lic String submitForm(@RequestParam("data")
String formData) {
```

```
    // Process the form data

    System.out.println("Received data: " +
formData);

    return "formSuccess"; // View name

  }

}
```

Accessing Request Data

Spring MVC provides several ways to access data from an HTTP request:

- @RequestParam: Retrieves the value of a request parameter. Request parameters are typically included in the URL's query string (for GET requests) or in the request body (for POST requests).
- @PathVariable: Retrieves the value of a path variable. Path variables are parts of the URL itself.

Java

```
import org.springframework.stereotype.Controller;

import
org.springframework.web.bind.annotation.GetMappin
g;

import
org.springframework.web.bind.annotation.PathVaria
ble;
```

```java
import
org.springframework.web.bind.annotation.RequestPa
ram;

import
org.springframework.web.servlet.ModelAndView;


@Controller

public class MyController {


    @GetMapping("/items/{itemId}")

    public ModelAndView
getItemDetails(@PathVariable("itemId") int
itemId) {

        ModelAndView modelAndView = new
ModelAndView("itemDetails");

        modelAndView.addObject("itemId", itemId);

        // Retrieve item details from database

        return modelAndView;

    }


    @GetMapping("/search")

    public ModelAndView
searchItems(@RequestParam("query") String query,
```

```java
@RequestParam(value = "page", defaultValue = "1")
int page) {

    ModelAndView modelAndView = new
ModelAndView("searchResults");

    modelAndView.addObject("query", query);

    modelAndView.addObject("page", page);

    // Perform search and retrieve results
from database

    return modelAndView;

  }

}
```

In this example:

- ○ @PathVariable("itemId") int itemId retrieves the value of the "itemId" path variable from the URL (e.g., /items/123).
- ○ @RequestParam(value = "page", defaultValue = "1") int page retrieves the value of the "page" request parameter. The value attribute specifies the parameter name, and the defaultValue attribute provides a default value if the parameter is not present in the request.
- • @RequestHeader: Retrieves the value of a request header. Request headers provide additional information about the request (e.g., user agent, content type).

Java

```java
import org.springframework.stereotype.Controller;

import org.springframework.web.bind.annotation.GetMapping;

import org.springframework.web.bind.annotation.RequestHeader;

import org.springframework.web.servlet.ModelAndView;


@Controller
public class MyController {


    @GetMapping("/info")
    public ModelAndView getRequestInfo(@RequestHeader("User-Agent") String userAgent) {

        ModelAndView modelAndView = new ModelAndView("requestInfo");

        modelAndView.addObject("userAgent", userAgent);

        return modelAndView;

    }

}
```

@RequestHeader("User-Agent") String userAgent retrieves the value of the "User-Agent" request header.

- **@CookieValue:** Retrieves the value of a cookie. Cookies are small pieces of data stored on the user's computer by the web server.

Java

```java
import org.springframework.stereotype.Controller;

import org.springframework.web.bind.annotation.CookieValue;

import org.springframework.web.bind.annotation.GetMapping;

import org.springframework.web.servlet.ModelAndView;



@Controller

public class MyController {


    @GetMapping("/preferences")

    public ModelAndView getPreferences(@CookieValue(value = "theme", defaultValue = "light") String theme) {
```

```java
        ModelAndView modelAndView = new
ModelAndView("preferences");

        modelAndView.addObject("theme", theme);

        return modelAndView;

    }

}
```

@CookieValue(value = "theme", defaultValue = "light") String theme retrieves the value of the "theme" cookie.

Constructing Responses

Controllers are responsible for constructing the HTTP response to be sent back to the client. In Spring MVC, you have several options for constructing responses:

- ModelAndView: This object holds both the data to be displayed (the model) and the name of the view to be used to render the response.

```java
Java


import org.springframework.stereotype.Controller;

import
org.springframework.web.bind.annotation.GetMappin
g;

import
org.springframework.web.servlet.ModelAndView;
```

```java
@Controller

public class MyController {


    @GetMapping("/data")

    public ModelAndView getData() {

        ModelAndView modelAndView = new
ModelAndView("dataView");

        modelAndView.addObject("data", "Some data
from the server");

        return modelAndView;

    }

}
```

- String: You can return a String representing the name of the
  view to be rendered.

import org.springframework.stereotype.Controller;

import org.springframework.ui.Model;

**import
org.springframework.web.bind.annotation.GetMapping;
2**

@Controller

public class MyController {

```java
@GetMapping("/message")

public String getMessage(Model model) {

    model.addAttribute("message", "A simple message");

    return "messageView";

}

}
```

```

```

In this case, Spring MVC will use the `Model` object to pass data to the view.

- **@ResponseBody:** This annotation indicates that the method's return value should be directly written to the HTTP response body, instead of being interpreted as a view name. This is commonly used for creating RESTful web services that return data in formats like JSON or XML.

Java

```java
import org.springframework.stereotype.Controller;

import org.springframework.web.bind.annotation.GetMapping;

import org.springframework.web.bind.annotation.ResponseBody;
```

```java
@Controller

public class MyController {


    @GetMapping("/api/data")

    @ResponseBody

    public String getDataAsJson() {

        return "{\"key\":\"value\"}"; // Returns
JSON data

    }

}
```

- ResponseEntity: This class allows you to have more control over the HTTP response, including setting the status code, headers, and body.

Java

```java
import org.springframework.http.HttpStatus;

import org.springframework.http.ResponseEntity;

import org.springframework.stereotype.Controller;

import
org.springframework.web.bind.annotation.GetMapping;
```

```java
@Controller

public class MyController {


    @GetMapping("/status")

    public ResponseEntity<String> getStatus() {

        return new ResponseEntity<>("OK",
HttpStatus.OK);

    }


    @GetMapping("/error")

    public ResponseEntity<String> getError() {

        return new ResponseEntity<>("Error
occurred", HttpStatus.INTERNAL_SERVER_ERROR);

    }

}
```

A real-world example:

Consider a REST API for an online store. You'd use @GetMapping, @PostMapping, @PutMapping, and @DeleteMapping to handle different types of requests (e.g., retrieving product information, creating a new order, updating a product). You'd use @PathVariable to access product IDs in the URL. You'd use @RequestBody to receive data in JSON format. And you'd use ResponseEntity to send back appropriate HTTP status codes (e.g., 200 for success, 404 for not found, 500 for server error).

Here's a practical exercise:

1. Create a Spring MVC controller with methods to handle different HTTP methods (GET, POST).
2. Use @RequestParam and @PathVariable to access data from the request.
3. Use @ResponseBody and ResponseEntity to construct different types of responses.
4. Experiment with setting different HTTP status codes and headers.

This exercise will give you hands-on experience with handling HTTP requests and responses in Spring MVC.

5.3 Working with Forms and Data Binding

Okay, let's discuss how Spring MVC simplifies working with HTML forms and the powerful concept of data binding. Handling forms is a crucial part of web development, as they're the primary way users interact with your application to submit data.

So, what's the challenge with forms? In a traditional web application, you'd have to manually extract each form field's value from the HTTP request, convert it to the appropriate data type, and then set the corresponding properties of your Java objects. This can be tedious and repetitive, especially for forms with many fields.

Spring MVC's data binding feature automates this process. It automatically populates Java objects with data from the HTTP request, saving you a lot of boilerplate code and reducing the risk of errors.

Data Binding in Spring MVC

Spring MVC's data binding mechanism relies on conventions and annotations. It works by matching the names of the form fields with the names of the properties of your Java objects.

Let's illustrate this with an example. Suppose we have a simple form to collect user information:

HTML

```
<form action="/processForm" method="post">

  <label for="name">Name:</label><br>

  <input type="text" id="name" name="name"><br>

  <label for="email">Email:</label><br>

  <input type="text" id="email"
name="email"><br><br>

  <input type="submit" value="Submit">

</form>
```

Here, the form has two input fields: "name" and "email."

Now, let's create a corresponding Java class to represent the user data:

Java

```
public class User {

    private String name;

    private String email;
```

```java
    public String getName() {

        return name;

    }


    public void setName(String name) {

        this.name = name;

    }


    public String getEmail() {

        return email;

    }


    public void setEmail(String email) {

        this.email = email;

    }

}
```

This User class has two properties: "name" and "email," with their corresponding getter and setter methods.

To enable data binding in our controller, we use the @ModelAttribute annotation:

```java
import org.springframework.stereotype.Controller;

import
org.springframework.web.bind.annotation.GetMapping;

import
org.springframework.web.bind.annotation.ModelAttribute;

import
org.springframework.web.bind.annotation.PostMapping;

import
org.springframework.web.servlet.ModelAndView;


@Controller
public class MyFormController {


    @GetMapping("/form")
    public ModelAndView showForm() {

        ModelAndView modelAndView = new
ModelAndView("userForm");

        modelAndView.addObject("user", new
User()); // Create an empty User object

        return modelAndView;
```

```
    }


    @PostMapping("/processForm")

    public ModelAndView
processForm(@ModelAttribute("user") User user) {

        ModelAndView modelAndView = new
ModelAndView("formResult");

        modelAndView.addObject("message",
"Received User Data: Name = " + user.getName() +
", Email = " + user.getEmail());

        return modelAndView;

    }

}
```

Let's break down this controller:

- @Controller: Marks the class as a controller.
- @GetMapping("/form"): Handles GET requests to the "/form" URL.
- showForm(): This method prepares the form for display. It creates a new, empty User object and adds it to the model with the key "user." This is important because the view will use this object to bind the form data.
- @PostMapping("/processForm"): Handles POST requests to the "/processForm" URL (which is the action attribute of our form).
- processForm(@ModelAttribute("user") User user): This is where the magic happens. The @ModelAttribute("user") annotation does two things:
  - It tells Spring MVC to create a User object.

- It tells Spring MVC to populate the properties of this User object with the values from the form fields. Spring MVC automatically matches the form field names ("name" and "email") with the User class's property names.
- The processForm method then processes the populated User object.

Here's how the view (userForm.html) might look (using Thymeleaf):

HTML

```
<!DOCTYPE HTML>

<html xmlns:th="http://www.thymeleaf.org">

<head>

    <title>User Form</title>

</head>

<body>

    <h1>Enter User Details</h1>

    <form action="/processForm" method="post"
th:object="${user}">

        <label for="name">Name:</label><br>

        <input type="text" id="name" name="name"
th:field="*{name}"><br>

        <label for="email">Email:</label><br>
```

```
        <input type="text" id="email"
name="email" th:field="*{email}"><br><br>

        <input type="submit" value="Submit">

    </form>

</body>

</html>
```

- th:object="${user}": This Thymeleaf attribute associates the form with the "user" object that we added to the model in the controller.
- th:field="*{name}" and th:field="*{email}": These Thymeleaf attributes bind the input fields to the "name" and "email" properties of the "user" object.

When the user submits the form, Spring MVC creates a User object and automatically sets its "name" and "email" properties based on the submitted form data. You don't have to write any code to do this manually!

Benefits of Data Binding

- Reduced Code: It significantly reduces the amount of code you need to write.
- Improved Readability: It makes your code cleaner and easier to understand.
- Increased Maintainability: It makes your code easier to maintain.
- Type Safety: It helps prevent type conversion errors.

Real-World Example

Consider a registration form on an e-commerce website. The form might collect user information like name, address, phone number, and password. Spring MVC's data binding can automatically populate a User object with this data, simplifying the registration process.

Practical Exercise

1. Create a Spring MVC application with a form to collect data for a custom object (e.g., a "Product" object with name, price, and description).
2. Use @ModelAttribute to bind the form data to the object.
3. Display the submitted data on a separate page.
4. Experiment with adding more fields to the form and the object.

This exercise will give you a solid understanding of how to use data binding to handle forms efficiently in Spring MVC.

5.4 View Technologies (JSP, Thymeleaf)

Okay, let's discuss view technologies in Spring MVC. The "view" in MVC is responsible for presenting the data to the user, and Spring MVC supports various technologies to help you build these views. It's important to choose the right technology for your project, as it significantly impacts how you structure and maintain your user interface.

So, what are view technologies? They are tools and frameworks that allow you to create dynamic web pages. They typically involve template engines that combine static HTML with dynamic data from your application. Spring MVC acts as the conductor, passing the data from the controller to the chosen view technology for rendering.

Let's look at two prominent options: JSP (JavaServer Pages) and Thymeleaf.

JSP (JavaServer Pages)

JSP is a technology that allows you to embed Java code within HTML pages. It's a mature technology that has been around for a while and is part of the Java EE specification.

Here's a simple example of a JSP page:

Java

```
<%@ page contentType="text/html;charset=UTF-8"
language="java" %>

<html>

<head>

    <title>Greeting</title>

</head>

<body>

    <h1>Greeting Page</h1>

    <% String message = (String)
request.getAttribute("message"); %>

    <p>Message: <%= message %></p>

</body>

</html>
```

In this JSP:

- <%@ page ... %>: This is a JSP directive that sets the content type and language.
- <% String message = (String) request.getAttribute("message"); %>: This is a scriptlet, a

block of Java code that can be executed on the server. Here, it retrieves the "message" attribute from the request.

- <%= message %>: This is an expression that outputs the value of the message variable.

When a request is made for a JSP page, the server executes the Java code within the JSP, generates HTML, and sends the resulting HTML to the browser.

Advantages of JSP:

- Mature Technology: It's a well-established technology with plenty of resources and community support.
- Java Integration: It provides direct access to Java code, which can be useful for complex logic.

Disadvantages of JSP:

- Mixing Logic and Presentation: It often leads to mixing business logic and presentation code, making the view harder to maintain and test.
- Debugging Challenges: Debugging JSP pages can sometimes be difficult.
- Expression Language Limitations: While JSP has an Expression Language (EL) to simplify data access, it can still be less expressive than other template engines.

Thymeleaf

Thymeleaf is a modern server-side Java template engine that's designed to be a natural way of creating HTML5 output. It emphasizes natural templating, meaning that your templates can be displayed correctly in browsers even without a server.

Here's the same greeting example using Thymeleaf:

HTML

```
<!DOCTYPE HTML>

<html xmlns:th="http://www.thymeleaf.org">

<head>

    <title>Greeting</title>

</head>

<body>

    <h1>Greeting Page</h1>

    <p th:text="${message}">This text will be
replaced by Thymeleaf</p>

</body>

</html>
```

In this Thymeleaf template:

- xmlns:th="http://www.thymeleaf.org": This declares the Thymeleaf namespace.
- th:text="${message}": This Thymeleaf attribute replaces the content of the <p> tag with the value of the "message" variable from the model.

Thymeleaf templates are valid HTML. If you open this file in a browser, you'll see "This text will be replaced by Thymeleaf" because the browser doesn't understand the th:text attribute. However, when processed by Thymeleaf on the server, it will correctly display the message.

Advantages of Thymeleaf:

- Natural Templating: Templates are valid HTML, making them easier for designers to work with.

- Stronger Separation of Concerns: It promotes a better separation of presentation and logic.
- Expressive Syntax: It has a rich and expressive syntax for accessing data, iterating over collections, and performing conditional logic.
- Spring Integration: It has excellent integration with Spring MVC.

Disadvantages of Thymeleaf:

- Learning Curve: It has its own syntax that you need to learn.

Choosing a View Technology

In modern Spring MVC applications, Thymeleaf is generally preferred over JSP. Its natural templating, stronger separation of concerns, and expressive syntax make it a better choice for building maintainable and robust web applications.

Configuring a View Resolver

Spring MVC uses a ViewResolver to determine which view technology to use. You need to configure a ViewResolver in your Spring configuration.

Here's an example of configuring a ThymeleafViewResolver in Java configuration:

```Java

import
org.springframework.context.annotation.Bean;

import
org.springframework.context.annotation.Configurat
ion;
```

```java
import
org.thymeleaf.spring5.SpringTemplateEngine;

import
org.thymeleaf.spring5.templateresolver.SpringReso
urceTemplateResolver;

import
org.thymeleaf.spring5.view.ThymeleafViewResolver;


@Configuration

public class ThymeleafConfig {


    @Bean

    public SpringResourceTemplateResolver
templateResolver() {

        SpringResourceTemplateResolver
templateResolver = new
SpringResourceTemplateResolver();


templateResolver.setPrefix("/WEB-INF/views/"); //
Location of your templates

        templateResolver.setSuffix(".html"); //
Template file extension

        templateResolver.setTemplateMode("HTML");

        templateResolver.setCacheable(true); //
Enable caching for performance
```

```java
        return templateResolver;

    }


    @Bean

    public SpringTemplateEngine templateEngine()
{

        SpringTemplateEngine templateEngine = new
SpringTemplateEngine();

templateEngine.setTemplateResolver(templateResolv
er());

templateEngine.setEnableSpringELCompiler(true);
// Enable Spring EL

        return templateEngine;

    }


    @Bean

    public ThymeleafViewResolver viewResolver() {

        ThymeleafViewResolver viewResolver = new
ThymeleafViewResolver();

viewResolver.setTemplateEngine(templateEngine());
```

```
viewResolver.setCharacterEncoding("UTF-8");

       return viewResolver;

   }

}
```

A real-world example:

Consider an e-commerce application. You would use a view technology (like Thymeleaf) to display product listings, product details, shopping carts, and order confirmation pages. The view technology would dynamically generate HTML based on the data from the model.

Here's a practical exercise:

1. Create a Spring MVC application that displays data from a simple model object (e.g., a list of products).
2. Implement the view using both JSP and Thymeleaf.
3. Compare the code and the resulting HTML.
4. Experiment with different Thymeleaf features, such as iteration and conditional logic.

This exercise will give you a hands-on understanding of how to use view technologies in Spring MVC and help you appreciate the benefits of Thymeleaf.

Chapter 6: Spring Data Access

So, you're building an application that needs to store and retrieve data? That's where Spring's data access features come in. Spring provides a comprehensive set of tools and abstractions to simplify database interaction, handling everything from basic JDBC to more advanced ORM (Object-Relational Mapping) techniques.

6.1 Understanding JDBC and Spring's Data Access Abstraction

Okay, let's talk about how Java applications interact with databases, starting with JDBC and then moving on to how Spring simplifies this process with its data access abstraction.

So, at the core of Java database interaction is JDBC, which stands for Java Database Connectivity. Think of JDBC as a bridge that allows your Java code to communicate with various relational databases. It's an API, a set of interfaces and classes, that provides a standard way to send SQL queries and receive results.

Here's a breakdown of what JDBC does:

1. Establishing a Connection: First, you need to establish a connection to the database. This involves providing the database's URL, your username, and your password. The URL specifies the location of the database and the driver to use.
2. Creating Statements: Once you have a connection, you can create statements to execute SQL queries. There are different types of statements:
    o Statement: For simple, static SQL queries.
    o PreparedStatement: For parameterized queries, which are more efficient and secure (prevent SQL injection).
    o CallableStatement: For calling stored procedures.

3. Executing Queries: You then execute the SQL query using the statement. This could be a SELECT query to retrieve data, or an INSERT, UPDATE, or DELETE query to modify data.

4. Processing Results: If you're executing a SELECT query, you'll receive a ResultSet object, which contains the data returned by the database. You need to iterate through the ResultSet to access the data.

5. Closing Resources: Finally, it's crucial to close the connection, statement, and ResultSet to release database resources.

Here's a simplified example of using JDBC to retrieve data:

Java

```java
import java.sql.Connection;

import java.sql.DriverManager;

import java.sql.ResultSet;

import java.sql.SQLException;

import java.sql.Statement;


public class JdbcExample {


    public static void main(String[] args) {
        String url =
"jdbc:mysql://localhost:3306/mydb"; // Replace
with your database URL

        String username = "user"; // Replace with
your database username
```

```java
        String password = "password"; // Replace
with your database password


        try (Connection connection =
DriverManager.getConnection(url, username,
password);
             Statement statement =
connection.createStatement();
             ResultSet resultSet =
statement.executeQuery("SELECT id, username FROM
users")) {


            while (resultSet.next()) {
                int id = resultSet.getInt("id");
                String usernameFromDb =
resultSet.getString("username");

                System.out.println("ID: " + id +
", Username: " + usernameFromDb);

            }


        } catch (SQLException e) {
            e.printStackTrace();
        }

    }

}
```

This code connects to a MySQL database, executes a SELECT query, and prints the ID and username of each user. The try-with-resources statement ensures that the connection, statement, and ResultSet are closed automatically.

While JDBC is powerful, it has some drawbacks:

- Boilerplate Code: You have to write a lot of repetitive code for connection management, statement creation, and result processing.
- Exception Handling: JDBC's SQLException is a checked exception, which forces you to handle it in every method that uses JDBC.
- Resource Management: You need to be careful to close database resources to avoid leaks.
- Data Mapping: You have to manually map data from the ResultSet to your Java objects.

This is where Spring's data access abstraction comes in. Spring provides a layer on top of JDBC to simplify these tasks. It handles much of the boilerplate code, resource management, and exception handling, allowing you to focus on writing your SQL queries and business logic.

Spring's core class for this is JdbcTemplate. It takes care of connection management, statement creation, and exception handling. You provide the SQL query and how to map the results, and JdbcTemplate does the rest.

Here's a simplified example using JdbcTemplate:

```java
Java

import
org.springframework.jdbc.core.JdbcTemplate;
import org.springframework.jdbc.core.RowMapper;
import org.springframework.stereotype.Repository;


import javax.sql.DataSource;
import java.sql.ResultSet;
```

```java
import java.sql.SQLException;

@Repository
public class UserDao {

    private final JdbcTemplate jdbcTemplate;

    public UserDao(DataSource dataSource) {
        this.jdbcTemplate = new
JdbcTemplate(dataSource);
    }

    public String getUsername(int userId) {
        String sql = "SELECT username FROM users
WHERE id = ?";
        return jdbcTemplate.queryForObject(sql,
String.class, userId);
    }

    public User getUser(int userId) {
        String sql = "SELECT id, username, email
FROM users WHERE id = ?";
        return jdbcTemplate.queryForObject(sql,
new RowMapper<User>() {
            @Override
            public User mapRow(ResultSet rs, int
rowNum) throws SQLException {
                User user = new User();
```

```
                    user.setId(rs.getInt("id"));

user.setUsername(rs.getString("username"));

user.setEmail(rs.getString("email"));
                    return user;
            }
        }, userId);
    }


    // Example User class (you'd have this
elsewhere)
    public static class User {
        private int id;
        private String username;
        private String email;

        // Getters and setters
        public int getId() { return id; }
        public void setId(int id) { this.id = id;
}
        public String getUsername() { return
username; }
        public void setUsername(String username)
{ this.username = username; }
        public String getEmail() { return email;
}
```

```
        public void setEmail(String email) {
this.email = email; }

    }

}
```

In this example:

- DataSource is a Spring interface for obtaining database connections. Spring provides implementations for various connection pooling technologies.
- JdbcTemplate is created with a DataSource.
- jdbcTemplate.queryForObject() is used to execute queries. The RowMapper interface is used to map rows from the ResultSet to User objects.

Spring's data access abstraction simplifies database interaction, making your code cleaner, more efficient, and easier to maintain. It handles many of the low-level details, allowing you to focus on your application's logic.

Here's a practical exercise:

1. Set up a simple database table with some data.
2. Create a Spring application and configure a DataSource (e.g., using Spring Boot's auto-configuration).
3. Use JdbcTemplate to perform basic CRUD (Create, Read, Update, Delete) operations on the table.
4. Experiment with different JdbcTemplate methods and RowMapper implementations.

This exercise will give you a good understanding of how Spring's data access abstraction simplifies JDBC programming.

6.2 Using Spring JDBC and NamedParameterJdbcTemplate

Okay, let's get more specific about how to use Spring JDBC, focusing on JdbcTemplate and its more powerful sibling, NamedParameterJdbcTemplate. These are your workhorses when you need fine-grained control over your database interactions within Spring.

So, as we discussed before, JdbcTemplate is Spring's central class for simplifying JDBC operations.

It handles the tedious parts of JDBC programming, such as:

- Establishing and closing connections: You don't have to worry about manually opening and closing database connections. Spring takes care of this, often using connection pooling for efficiency.
- Creating and closing statements: JdbcTemplate creates and closes Statement or PreparedStatement objects, freeing you from this responsibility.
- Handling exceptions: It catches SQLExceptions and translates them into Spring's more general DataAccessException hierarchy, making exception handling more consistent.

This leaves you to focus on writing your SQL queries and processing the results.

Here's a closer look at how to use JdbcTemplate:

1. Setting up JdbcTemplate

You need to provide JdbcTemplate with a DataSource. A DataSource is a Spring interface for obtaining database connections. Spring provides various implementations, often leveraging connection pooling libraries like HikariCP for performance.

Here's how you might set it up in a Spring configuration:

Java

```
  import
org.springframework.context.annotation.Bean;

import
org.springframework.context.annotation.Configurat
ion;

import
org.springframework.jdbc.core.JdbcTemplate;

import javax.sql.DataSource;


@Configuration

public class AppConfig {


    @Bean

    public JdbcTemplate jdbcTemplate(DataSource
dataSource) {

        return new JdbcTemplate(dataSource);

    }
```

```
// Configure your DataSource here (e.g.,
using Spring Boot's auto-configuration)

}
```

In a Spring Boot application, much of this configuration is handled automatically.

2. Executing Queries

JdbcTemplate provides a rich set of methods for executing different types of SQL queries:

- queryForObject(): Retrieves a single object from the database. It's useful for queries that are expected to return one row and one column.

Java

```
public String getUsername(int userId) {

    String sql = "SELECT username FROM users
WHERE id = ?";

    return jdbcTemplate.queryForObject(sql,
String.class, userId);

}
```

Here, String.class specifies the expected return type.

- queryForList(): Retrieves a list of maps, where each map represents a row from the result set.

Java

```java
public List<Map<String, Object>> getUsers() {

    String sql = "SELECT id, username, email FROM
users";

    return jdbcTemplate.queryForList(sql);

}
```

- query(): Retrieves a list of objects, allowing you to map each row to a custom Java object using a RowMapper.

Java

```java
import org.springframework.jdbc.core.RowMapper;

import java.sql.ResultSet;

import java.sql.SQLException;


public List<User> getUsers() {

    String sql = "SELECT id, username, email FROM
users";

    return jdbcTemplate.query(sql, new
RowMapper<User>() {

        @Override

        public User mapRow(ResultSet rs, int
rowNum) throws SQLException {

            User user = new User();
```

```java
        user.setId(rs.getInt("id"));

user.setUsername(rs.getString("username"));

        user.setEmail(rs.getString("email"));

        return user;

    }

  });

}
```

The RowMapper interface is crucial for mapping database rows to your application's objects.

- update(): Executes INSERT, UPDATE, or DELETE statements.

Java

```java
public int updateUserEmail(int userId, String newEmail) {

    String sql = "UPDATE users SET email = ? WHERE id = ?";

    return jdbcTemplate.update(sql, newEmail, userId);

}
```

This method returns the number of rows affected by the update.

NamedParameterJdbcTemplate

While JdbcTemplate uses ? placeholders for parameters, NamedParameterJdbcTemplate allows you to use named parameters in your SQL queries. This significantly improves readability and maintainability, especially for complex queries.

Here's how it works:

1. Setting up NamedParameterJdbcTemplate:
2. It's set up similarly to JdbcTemplate, but you use the NamedParameterJdbcTemplate class.

import org.springframework.context.annotation.Bean;

import org.springframework.context.annotation.Configuration;

import1 org.springframework.jdbc.core.namedparam.NamedParameterJdbcTemplate;

import javax.sql.DataSource;

```
@Configuration

public class AppConfig {


    @Bean

    public NamedParameterJdbcTemplate
namedParameterJdbcTemplate(DataSource dataSource)
{

        return new
NamedParameterJdbcTemplate(dataSource);
```

```
    }

  }

  ` ` `
```

Using Named Parameters:

You pass parameters to the query using a Map where the keys are the parameter names.

```java
Java

import
org.springframework.jdbc.core.namedparam.MapSqlPa
rameterSource;

import
org.springframework.jdbc.core.namedparam.NamedPar
ameterJdbcTemplate;

import org.springframework.stereotype.Repository;



@Repository

public class UserDao {


    private final NamedParameterJdbcTemplate
namedParameterJdbcTemplate;
```

```java
    public UserDao(NamedParameterJdbcTemplate
namedParameterJdbcTemplate) {

        this.namedParameterJdbcTemplate =
namedParameterJdbcTemplate;

    }


    public String getUsername(int userId) {

        String sql = "SELECT username FROM users
WHERE id = :userId";

        MapSqlParameterSource params = new
MapSqlParameterSource();

        params.addValue("userId", userId);

        return
namedParameterJdbcTemplate.queryForObject(sql,
params, String.class);

    }


    public int updateUserEmail(int userId, String
newEmail) {

        String sql = "UPDATE users SET email =
:email WHERE id = :id";

        MapSqlParameterSource params = new
MapSqlParameterSource();

        params.addValue("email", newEmail);
```

```
    params.addValue("id", userId);

    return
namedParameterJdbcTemplate.update(sql, params);

    }

}
```

Notice how the SQL query uses :userId and :email instead of ?. This makes it clear what each parameter represents.

Real-World Example

Consider a search functionality in an e-commerce application. You might need to construct complex SQL queries with multiple optional search criteria (e.g., product name, category, price range). NamedParameterJdbcTemplate is very helpful in this scenario because you can easily add or remove parameters without changing the order of the placeholders in the query.

Practical Exercise

1. Set up a database table with sample data.
2. Create a Spring application and configure a DataSource and JdbcTemplate (or NamedParameterJdbcTemplate).
3. Implement methods in a DAO (Data Access Object) to perform various database operations:
   - Retrieve data using queryForObject() and query().
   - Insert, update, and delete data using update().
   - Use NamedParameterJdbcTemplate for queries with multiple parameters.
4. Experiment with different ways to map results using RowMapper.

This exercise will solidify your understanding of Spring JDBC and its powerful features.

6.3 Introduction to Spring Data JPA and Repositories

Okay, let's move on to a higher level of data access abstraction in Spring: Spring Data JPA. This is where things get really interesting and where Spring significantly simplifies database interactions, especially when working with Object-Relational Mapping (ORM).

So, what is JPA? JPA, or Java Persistence API, is the Java standard for ORM. ORM is a technique that lets you interact with your database using objects instead of SQL. It handles the mapping between your Java objects and the database tables, so you don't have to write a lot of boilerplate code to convert data back and forth.

JPA defines specifications for:

- Entities: Java classes that represent database tables.
- Persistence Units: Configurations that define how to connect to the database.
- EntityManager: An API for performing database operations (like saving, retrieving, updating, and deleting entities).
- JPQL (Java Persistence Query Language): An object-oriented query language for querying entities.

However, even with JPA, you still have to write some code to interact with the EntityManager. This is where Spring Data JPA comes in.

Spring Data JPA takes JPA a step further by introducing the concept of repositories. A repository is an interface that defines methods for accessing data. Spring Data JPA automatically generates the implementation of these interfaces for you! This means you can focus on defining *what* data access operations you need, not *how* to implement them.

Let's break this down with an example.

Suppose we have a User entity:

Java

```java
import javax.persistence.Entity;

import javax.persistence.GeneratedValue;

import javax.persistence.GenerationType;

import javax.persistence.Id;


@Entity

public class User {


    @Id

    @GeneratedValue(strategy =
GenerationType.IDENTITY)

    private Long id;


    private String username;

    private String email;


    // Getters and setters (omitted for brevity)

    public Long getId() {
```

```java
        return id;

    }


    public void setId(Long id) {

        this.id = id;

    }


    public String getUsername() {

        return username;

    }


    public void setUsername(String username) {

        this.username = username;

    }


    public String getEmail() {

        return email;

    }


    public void setEmail(String email) {
```

```
        this.email = email;


    }



}
```

- @Entity:[1] This JPA annotation marks the User class as an entity, meaning it represents a table in the database.
- @Id: This annotation marks the id field as the primary key of the table.
- @GeneratedValue(strategy = GenerationType.IDENTITY): This annotation specifies that the primary key[2] should be generated automatically by the database.

Now, let's create a repository interface for accessing User entities:

Java

```java
import
org.springframework.data.jpa.repository.JpaReposi
tory;

import org.springframework.stereotype.Repository;



@Repository

public interface UserRepository extends
JpaRepository<User, Long> {



    User findByUsername(String username);
```

```
    // You can define other custom query methods
here

}
```

- @Repository: This Spring annotation marks this interface as a repository, making it a Spring bean.
- JpaRepository<User, Long>: This is the magic. JpaRepository is a Spring Data JPA interface that provides basic CRUD (Create, Read, Update, Delete) operations for the User entity. The <User, Long> type parameters specify the entity type (User) and the type of its primary key (Long).
- User findByUsername(String username);: This is a custom query method. Spring Data JPA automatically generates the implementation for this method based on its name. It understands that you want to find a user by their username.

To use this repository, you simply inject it into your service or controller:

```
Java

import
org.springframework.beans.factory.annotation.Auto
wired;

import org.springframework.stereotype.Service;


@Service

public class UserService {
```

```java
    private final UserRepository userRepository;


    @Autowired

    public UserService(UserRepository
userRepository) {

        this.userRepository = userRepository;

    }


    public User getUser(Long id) {

        return
userRepository.findById(id).orElse(null); //
JpaRepository provides findById

    }


    public User getUserByUsername(String
username) {

        return
userRepository.findByUsername(username); // Our
custom method

    }


    public void saveUser(User user) {
```

```
        userRepository.save(user); //
JpaRepository provides save

    }


    // ... other methods

}
```

Notice how little code we had to write! Spring Data JPA handles all the database interaction behind the scenes.

Benefits of Spring Data JPA and Repositories:

- Reduced Boilerplate Code: You don't have to write repetitive code for common database operations.
- Improved Readability: Your data access code becomes cleaner and easier to understand.
- Increased Productivity: You can develop data access layers much faster.
- Simplified Testing: Repositories are easy to mock and test.

Real-World Example:

Consider an online store application. You'd have entities like Product, Order, Customer, etc. Spring Data JPA repositories would allow you to easily perform operations like:

- Find all products in a category.
- Find orders placed by a customer.
- Save a new customer.

Practical Exercise:

1. Set up a database and define a few JPA entities.
2. Create Spring Data JPA repository interfaces for these entities.

3. Inject these repositories into a service class.
4. Implement methods in the service class to perform various database operations using the repositories.
5. Experiment with different methods provided by JpaRepository and define your own custom query methods.

This exercise will give you a strong foundation in Spring Data JPA and repositories, showing you how much they simplify data access in Spring applications.

6.4 Transaction Management in Spring

Okay, let's talk about transaction management in Spring. This is a crucial aspect of building reliable applications, especially when dealing with databases. It's about ensuring data consistency and integrity, and Spring provides powerful tools to handle it.

So, what is a transaction? In simple terms, a transaction is a sequence of database operations that should be treated as a single unit of work. Think of it like a series of steps that must all succeed or all fail together.

To understand why transactions are so important, let's consider a classic example: transferring money between bank accounts.

This involves two operations:

1. Deducting the amount from the sender's account.
2. Adding the amount to the recipient's account.

We want to make sure that these two operations happen atomically. That is, either both operations succeed, or neither of them does. If the first operation succeeds (money is deducted from the sender's account) but the second operation fails (money is not credited to the recipient's account), we end up with an inconsistent state – money disappears!

Transactions help us prevent such inconsistencies by ensuring the ACID properties:

- Atomicity: The entire transaction is treated as a single, indivisible unit. Either all changes within the transaction are applied, or none of them are. It's an "all or nothing" approach.
- Consistency: A transaction brings the database from one valid state to another valid state. It ensures that the database rules and constraints are not violated.
- Isolation: Transactions are isolated from each other. Concurrent transactions should not interfere with each other's results. This prevents issues like "dirty reads" (reading uncommitted data) and "lost updates" (one transaction's changes overwriting another's).
- Durability: Once a transaction is committed (successfully completed), the changes are permanent, even if the system crashes.

Now, how does Spring help with transaction management? Spring provides a powerful abstraction that simplifies transaction handling. It offers both programmatic and declarative transaction management.

- Programmatic Transaction Management: This involves explicitly writing code to begin, commit, and rollback transactions. While it gives you fine-grained control, it can lead to more verbose code.
- Declarative Transaction Management: This is the more common and preferred approach in Spring. It allows you to define transaction boundaries using configuration (usually with annotations), and Spring takes care of the actual transaction handling. This keeps your business logic code clean and focused.

Let's focus on declarative transaction management, as it's the most widely used. Spring uses AOP (Aspect-Oriented Programming) to implement declarative transaction management.

The key annotation for declarative transaction management is @Transactional. You can apply this annotation to methods or classes to indicate that they should be executed within a transaction.

Here's a simple example:

Java

```java
import org.springframework.stereotype.Service;

import
org.springframework.transaction.annotation.Transa
ctional;



@Service

public class MyService {


    @Transactional

    public void performOperations() {

        // Database operation 1

        // Database operation 2

        // Database operation 3

    }
```

```
}
```

In this code:

- @Service: This annotation marks MyService as a service component, which is a Spring bean.
- @Transactional: This annotation on the performOperations() method tells Spring to manage transactions for this method. When this method is called, Spring will:
  - Begin a transaction before the method execution.
  - Commit the transaction if the method completes successfully (without throwing an exception).
  - Rollback the transaction if the method throws an unchecked exception.

Spring also provides various attributes for the @Transactional annotation to fine-tune transaction behavior:

- propagation: Defines how a transaction should propagate when a method calls another transactional method. Common values include:
  - Propagation.REQUIRED (default): If a transaction exists, join it. If not, create a new one.
  - Propagation.REQUIRES_NEW: Always create a new transaction, suspending the current one if it exists.
  - Propagation.NESTED: Create a nested transaction (if supported by the database).
- isolation: Defines the isolation level of the transaction, which controls how concurrent transactions interact. Common values include:
  - Isolation.DEFAULT: Use the default isolation level of the database.
  - Isolation.READ_COMMITTED: Prevents dirty reads (reading uncommitted data).

- ○ Isolation.REPEATABLE_READ: Prevents non-repeatable reads (reading the same data multiple times with different results).
- ○ Isolation.SERIALIZABLE: The highest isolation level, preventing most concurrency issues.
- timeout: Specifies the timeout for the transaction in seconds.
- readOnly: Optimizes read-only transactions.
- rollbackFor: Specifies which exceptions should trigger a rollback.
- noRollbackFor: Specifies which exceptions should *not* trigger a rollback.

Here's a more complex example:

Java

```java
import org.springframework.stereotype.Service;

import org.springframework.transaction.annotation.Transactional;

import org.springframework.transaction.annotation.Propagation;

import org.springframework.transaction.annotation.Isolation;


@Service

public class MyService {
```

```
    @Transactional(propagation =
Propagation.REQUIRED, isolation =
Isolation.READ_COMMITTED, timeout = 10,
rollbackFor = Exception.class)

    public void transferFunds(String fromAccount,
String toAccount, double amount) {

        // Deduct amount from fromAccount

        // Add amount to toAccount

    }



    @Transactional(propagation =
Propagation.REQUIRES_NEW)

    public void logTransaction(String
transactionDetails) {

        // Log the transaction details

    }

}
```

In this example:

- @Transactional(propagation = Propagation.REQUIRED, isolation = Isolation.READ_COMMITTED, timeout = 10, rollbackFor = Exception.class): This annotation specifies that the transferFunds() method should run in a transaction. If a transaction already exists, it will join it. It sets the isolation level to READ_COMMITTED, the timeout to 10 seconds, and specifies that any Exception should trigger a rollback.

- @Transactional(propagation = Propagation.REQUIRES_NEW): This annotation specifies that the logTransaction() method should always run in a new transaction, even if there's an existing transaction.

Real-World Example:

Consider an e-commerce application. When a user places an order, several database operations might be involved:

- Creating a new order record.
- Updating product inventory.
- Creating payment records.
- Sending confirmation emails.

These operations should be performed atomically. If any operation fails, the entire order process should be rolled back to maintain data consistency. Spring's declarative transaction management simplifies handling these complex scenarios.

Practical Exercise:

1. Set up a database with a few tables and relationships.
2. Create a Spring application and configure a DataSource and a PlatformTransactionManager (e.g., DataSourceTransactionManager for JDBC).
3. Implement a service with methods that perform multiple database operations.
4. Use the @Transactional annotation to manage transactions in these methods.
5. Experiment with different @Transactional attributes (propagation, isolation, rollbackFor, etc.) to understand their behavior.
6. Simulate failures during database operations and verify that transactions are rolled back correctly.

This exercise will provide you with a solid understanding of transaction management in Spring and how to use @Transactional effectively.

Chapter 7: Spring RESTful Web Services

So, you want to build APIs? Great! RESTful web services are the standard way for applications to communicate over the web, and Spring provides excellent support for building them.

7.1 Building RESTful APIs with Spring MVC

Okay, let's talk about building RESTful APIs using Spring MVC. You already know that Spring MVC is Spring's framework for building web applications, but it's also incredibly powerful for creating APIs that communicate over the web. The key difference is that instead of returning HTML to be rendered in a browser, RESTful APIs primarily return data, often in JSON or XML format, for other applications to consume.

So, what are RESTful APIs? REST stands for Representational State Transfer. It's an architectural style for designing networked applications. RESTful[1] APIs adhere to certain principles that make them scalable, flexible, and easy to use.

Here are some of the key principles of REST:

- Stateless: Each request from a client to a server must contain all the information necessary to understand the request, and cannot take advantage of any stored context on the server. This[2] means the server doesn't "remember" anything about previous requests.
- Client-Server: The client and server operate independently. The client initiates requests, and the server responds.
- Cacheable: Responses should be cacheable whenever possible to improve performance.

- Layered System: The architecture can be composed of layers (e.g., a proxy server) without the client needing to know about them.
- Uniform Interface: This is the most crucial principle. It defines a consistent way for clients to interact with the server. The uniform interface includes:
  - Resource Identification: Resources are identified by URLs (Uniform Resource Locators). For example, /users might represent a collection of users, and /users/123 might represent a specific user with ID 123.
  - Resource Manipulation through Representations: Clients manipulate resources by sending representations of those resources in the request body (e.g., JSON data representing a new user).
  - Self-descriptive Messages: Responses include metadata (e.g., HTTP headers) to provide information about the response.
  - Hypermedia as the Engine of Application State (HATEOAS): Responses may include links to related resources, allowing clients to navigate the API dynamically. (This is a more advanced concept, and we won't focus on it heavily here)

Now, how does Spring MVC help us build these RESTful APIs? It provides annotations and classes that simplify handling HTTP requests and constructing responses.

Key Spring MVC Components for REST APIs

1. @RestController: This is a convenience annotation that combines @Controller and @ResponseBody.
   - @Controller: As you know, this annotation marks a class as a controller, responsible for handling web requests.

- @ResponseBody: This annotation, when applied to a method, indicates that the method's return value should be directly written to the HTTP response body. This is crucial for REST APIs, where you typically return data (like JSON) instead of a view name.
- By using @RestController, you don't need to annotate every method with @ResponseBody. It's a handy shortcut.

2. @RequestMapping, @GetMapping, @PostMapping, @PutMapping, @DeleteMapping: These annotations are used to map HTTP requests to controller methods.
   - @RequestMapping: This is the most versatile annotation, allowing you to specify the URL path, HTTP method, and other criteria for mapping requests.
   - @GetMapping: A shorthand for @RequestMapping(method = RequestMethod.GET), used to map GET requests (used for retrieving data).
   - @PostMapping: A shorthand for @RequestMapping(method = RequestMethod.POST), used to map POST requests (used for creating new resources).
   - @PutMapping: A shorthand for @RequestMapping(method = RequestMethod.PUT), used to map PUT requests (used for updating existing resources).
   - @DeleteMapping: A shorthand for @RequestMapping(method = RequestMethod.DELETE), used to map DELETE requests (used for deleting resources).

3. @PathVariable: This annotation is used to extract values from the URL path. For example, if you have a URL like /users/123, you can use @PathVariable to get the value "123" (the user ID).

4. @RequestBody: This annotation is used to access the data sent in the request body. For example, if a client sends JSON data representing a new user in a POST request, you can use @RequestBody to have Spring automatically convert that JSON data into a Java object.
5. ResponseEntity: This class provides more control over the HTTP response, allowing you to set the status code, headers, and body.

A Complete Example

Let's build a simple REST API for managing users:

Java

```java
import org.springframework.web.bind.annotation.*;

import org.springframework.http.ResponseEntity;

import org.springframework.http.HttpStatus;

import java.util.*;


@RestController

@RequestMapping("/users")

public class UserController {


    private final List<User> users = new
ArrayList<>();

    private int nextId = 1;
```

```java
@GetMapping

public ResponseEntity<List<User>>
getAllUsers() {

    return ResponseEntity.ok(users); //
Returns all users with a 200 OK status

}


@GetMapping("/{id}")

public ResponseEntity<User>
getUserById(@PathVariable int id) {

    Optional<User> user =
users.stream().filter(u -> u.getId() ==
id).findFirst();

    if (user.isPresent()) {

        return ResponseEntity.ok(user.get());
// Returns the user with a 200 OK status

    } else {

        return
ResponseEntity.notFound().build(); // Returns a
404 Not Found status

    }

}
```

```java
@PostMapping

public ResponseEntity<User>
createUser(@RequestBody User user) {

    user.setId(nextId++);

    users.add(user);

    return
ResponseEntity.status(HttpStatus.CREATED).body(us
er); // Returns the created user with a 201
Created status

}


@PutMapping("/{id}")

public ResponseEntity<User>
updateUser(@PathVariable int id, @RequestBody
User updatedUser) {

    for (int i = 0; i < users.size(); i++) {

        if (users.get(i).getId() == id) {

            updatedUser.setId(id);

            users.set(i, updatedUser);

            return
ResponseEntity.ok(updatedUser); // Returns the
updated user with a 200 OK status

        }

    }
```

```java
        return ResponseEntity.notFound().build();
// Returns a 404 Not Found status

    }


    @DeleteMapping("/{id}")

    public ResponseEntity<Void>
deleteUser(@PathVariable int id) {

        users.removeIf(user -> user.getId() ==
id);

        return
ResponseEntity.noContent().build(); // Returns a
204 No Content status

    }

}


class User {

    private int id;

    private String name;

    private String email;


    // Constructors, getters, and setters
(omitted for brevity)

    public User() {}
```

```java
    public User(int id, String name, String
email) {

        this.id = id;

        this.name = name;

        this.email = email;

    }


    public int getId() {

        return id;

    }


    public void setId(int id) {

        this.id = id;

    }


    public String getName() {

        return name;

    }


    public void setName(String name) {
```

```java
        this.name = name;

    }



    public String getEmail() {

        return email;

    }



    public void setEmail(String email) {

        this.email = email;

    }

}
```

In this example:

- @RestController and @RequestMapping("/users"): We're defining a controller that handles requests to the /users endpoint.
- @GetMapping: We use @GetMapping to handle GET requests for retrieving users.
- @PathVariable: We use @PathVariable to extract the user ID from the URL (e.g., /users/123).
- @PostMapping: We use @PostMapping to handle POST requests for creating new users. @RequestBody is used to convert the JSON data sent in the request body to a User object.
- @PutMapping: We use @PutMapping to handle PUT requests for updating existing users.
- @DeleteMapping: We use @DeleteMapping to handle DELETE requests for deleting users.

- ResponseEntity: We use ResponseEntity to return appropriate HTTP status codes (e.g., 200 OK, 201 Created, 404 Not Found, 204 No Content).

Real-World Example

Consider an online bookstore. You could build a REST API to allow clients to:

- Retrieve information about books (GET /books, GET /books/{id}).
- Search for books (GET /books/search?query=...).
- Create new books (POST /books).
- Update book information (PUT /books/{id}).
- Delete books (DELETE /books/{id}).

Practical Exercise

1. Design a simple REST API for a specific domain (e.g., a to-do list, a library, a blog).
2. Create a Spring MVC controller with methods to handle different HTTP methods (GET, POST, PUT, DELETE) for your API.
3. Use @RequestMapping, @GetMapping, @PostMapping, @PutMapping, and @DeleteMapping to map requests to controller methods.
4. Use @PathVariable and @RequestBody to access data from the request.
5. Use ResponseEntity to construct appropriate responses with correct HTTP status codes.

This exercise will give you a solid foundation in building RESTful APIs with Spring MVC.

7.2 *Working with JSON and XML*

Okay, let's talk about how Spring MVC handles data formats like JSON and XML, which are very common in RESTful APIs. When building APIs, you're not just dealing with HTML to be displayed in a browser; you're often exchanging data between applications, and formats like JSON and XML are crucial for that.

So, why are JSON and XML important?

- JSON (JavaScript Object Notation): It's a lightweight, human-readable format for representing data. It's based on JavaScript object syntax but is used by many programming languages. It's very popular in web APIs due to its simplicity and efficiency.
- XML (Extensible Markup Language): It's a more verbose format than JSON but provides more structure and flexibility. While less common than JSON in modern web APIs, it's still used in some enterprise systems.

Spring MVC provides excellent support for working with both JSON and XML, making it easy to send and receive data in these formats.

Handling JSON

Spring MVC primarily uses the Jackson library to handle JSON conversion. Jackson is a high-performance JSON processor for Java. The good news is that Spring Boot often includes Jackson by default, so you usually don't need to add any extra dependencies to your project.

Here's how Spring MVC handles JSON:

1. Serialization (Java to JSON): When a controller method needs to return data as JSON, Spring MVC uses Jackson to convert the Java object into its JSON representation.

2. Deserialization (JSON to Java): When a controller method receives JSON data in the request body (e.g., from a POST or PUT request), Spring MVC uses Jackson to convert the JSON data into a Java object.

The key annotation here is @ResponseBody. When you annotate a controller method with @ResponseBody, you're telling Spring MVC to write the method's return value directly to the HTTP response body, and Spring MVC will use an appropriate HttpMessageConverter to perform the conversion.

If Jackson is available, Spring MVC will automatically use the MappingJackson2HttpMessageConverter to handle JSON conversion.

Here's an example:

Java

```java
import org.springframework.web.bind.annotation.*;

import java.util.ArrayList;

import java.util.List;



@RestController

@RequestMapping("/products")

public class ProductController {


    private final List<Product> products = new
ArrayList<>();
```

```java
    public ProductController() {

        products.add(new Product(1, "Laptop",
1200.00));

        products.add(new Product(2, "Keyboard",
75.00));

    }


    @GetMapping

    public List<Product> getAllProducts() {

        return products; // Spring converts this
list to JSON

    }


    @PostMapping

    public Product createProduct(@RequestBody
Product product) {

        products.add(product); // Spring converts
the incoming JSON to a Product object

        return product;

    }

}
```

```java
class Product {

    private int id;

    private String name;

    private double price;


    // Constructors, getters, and setters

    public Product() {}


    public Product(int id, String name, double
price) {

        this.id = id;

        this.name = name;

        this.price = price;

    }


    public int getId() {

        return id;

    }


    public void setId(int id) {

        this.id = id;
```

```java
    }


    public String getName() {

        return name;

    }


    public void setName(String name) {

        this.name = name;

    }


    public double getPrice() {

        return price;

    }


    public void setPrice(double price) {

        this.price = price;

    }

}
```

In this example:

- @RestController: This annotation combines @Controller and @ResponseBody, so the return values of the methods are automatically converted to JSON.

- @GetMapping: When you make a GET request to /products, Spring MVC uses Jackson to convert the List<Product> to JSON and sends it in the response.
- @PostMapping: When you make a POST request to /products with JSON data in the request body, Spring MVC uses Jackson to convert the JSON data into a Product object.

Handling XML

Spring MVC can also handle XML, though it's less common than JSON in modern web APIs. To work with XML, you typically need to add a dependency for a library like JAXB (Java Architecture for XML Binding).

Here's a simplified example:

First, you need to add the JAXB dependency to your pom.xml (if you're using Maven):

XML

```
<dependency>

    <groupId>jakarta.xml.bind</groupId>

    <artifactId>jakarta.xml.bind-api</artifactId>

    <version>4.0.0</version>

</dependency>


<dependency>

    <groupId>org.glassfish.jaxb</groupId>
```

```xml
<artifactId>jaxb-runtime</artifactId>

<version>4.0.2</version>

</dependency>
```

Then, you need to annotate your Java class with JAXB annotations to define how it should be mapped to XML:

Java

```java
import javax.xml.bind.annotation.XmlRootElement;

import javax.xml.bind.annotation.XmlAttribute;


@XmlRootElement(name = "product")

class Product {


    private int id;

    private String name;

    private double price;


    // Constructors, getters, and setters


    public Product() {}
```

```java
    public Product(int id, String name, double
price) {

        this.id = id;

        this.name = name;

        this.price = price;

    }


    @XmlAttribute

    public int getId() {

        return id;

    }


    public void setId(int id) {

        this.id = id;

    }


    public String getName() {

        return name;

    }


    public void setName(String name) {
```

```java
        this.name = name;

    }


    public double getPrice() {

        return price;

    }


    public void setPrice(double price) {

        this.price = price;

    }

}
```

- @XmlRootElement(name = "product"): This annotation specifies the root element name in the XML document.
- @XmlAttribute: This annotation maps the id field to an XML attribute.

Here's a controller example:

Java

```java
import org.springframework.web.bind.annotation.*;

import java.util.ArrayList;

import java.util.List;
```

```java
@RestController

@RequestMapping("/products")

public class ProductController {


    private final List<Product> products = new
ArrayList<>();


    public ProductController() {

        products.add(new Product(1, "Laptop",
1200.00));

        products.add(new Product(2, "Keyboard",
75.00));

    }


    @GetMapping(produces = "application/xml")

    public List<Product> getAllProducts() {

        return products; // Spring converts this
list to XML

    }


    @PostMapping(consumes = "application/xml")

    public Product createProduct(@RequestBody
Product product) {
```

```
        products.add(product); // Spring converts
the incoming XML to a Product object

        return product;

    }

}
```

- @GetMapping(produces = "application/xml"): This specifies that the method produces XML.
- @PostMapping(consumes = "application/xml"): This specifies that the method consumes XML.

Content Negotiation

Spring MVC also supports content negotiation, which allows your API to serve different formats (JSON, XML) based on the client's request. Clients can use the Accept header in their requests to specify their preferred format.

Real-World Example

Imagine an API for a weather service. Clients might request weather data in JSON for use in a mobile app or in XML for integration with another system. Spring MVC's content negotiation capabilities allow you to support both.

Practical Exercise

1. Create a Spring MVC REST API that handles a simple entity (e.g., a "Book" with title, author, and ISBN).
2. Implement methods to retrieve and create these entities.
3. Use @ResponseBody and @RequestBody to handle JSON data.
4. (Optional) Add JAXB dependencies and annotations to handle XML as well.

5. Experiment with content negotiation to serve both JSON and XML based on the Accept header.

This exercise will give you a practical understanding of how to work with JSON and XML in Spring MVC REST APIs.

7.3 Handling HTTP Status Codes and Error Handling

Okay, let's talk about a crucial aspect of building robust RESTful APIs: handling HTTP status codes and errors. In a well-designed API, it's not enough to just return data; you also need to provide clear and informative feedback to the client about the outcome of their requests. HTTP status codes play a vital role in this.

So, what are HTTP status codes? They are three-digit codes returned by the server in response to a client's request. They provide a standardized way to communicate the result of the request. Think of them as a universal language between the client and the server.

Spring MVC provides excellent support for setting these status codes and handling errors gracefully.

HTTP Status Code Categories

HTTP status codes are divided into five categories:

- 1xx (Informational): These codes indicate that the request was received and is being processed. You rarely encounter these in typical API responses.
- 2xx (Success): These codes indicate that the request was successful.
- 3xx (Redirection): These codes indicate that the client needs to take further action to complete the request (e.g., redirect to a different URL).

- 4xx (Client Error): These codes indicate that there was an error on the client's side (e.g., invalid request, unauthorized access).
- 5xx (Server Error): These codes indicate that there was an error on the server's side.

Common HTTP Status Codes in REST APIs

Here are some of the most common status codes you'll use when building REST APIs:

- 200 OK: The request was successful, and the response contains the requested data. This is the most common status code for successful GET requests.
- 201 Created: The request was successful, and a new resource was created. This is typically used for successful POST requests. The response should ideally include the URL of the newly created resource in the Location header.
- 204 No Content: The request was successful, but there is no content to return in the response body. This is often used for successful DELETE requests.
- 400 Bad Request: The request was invalid. This could be due to missing required parameters, invalid data format, or other client-side errors.
- 401 Unauthorized: Authentication is required to access the requested resource. The client needs to provide valid credentials.
- 403 Forbidden: The client is authenticated but does not have permission to access the requested resource.
- 404 Not Found: The requested resource[1] was not found on the server.[2]
- 409 Conflict: The request could not be completed due to a conflict with the current state of the resource (e.g., trying to create a resource[3] with an ID that already exists).
- 500 Internal Server Error: An unexpected error occurred on the server while processing the request. This is a generic

error code and should be avoided if you can provide a more specific error code.

Using ResponseEntity in Spring MVC

Spring MVC provides the ResponseEntity class to give you fine-grained control over the HTTP response. It allows you to set the status code, headers, and body of the response.

Here's how you can use it:

Java

```
import org.springframework.http.HttpStatus;

import org.springframework.http.ResponseEntity;

import org.springframework.web.bind.annotation.*;

import java.util.ArrayList;

import java.util.List;

import java.util.Optional;


@RestController

@RequestMapping("/products")

public class ProductController {


    private final List<Product> products = new
ArrayList<>();
```

```java
public ProductController() {

        products.add(new Product(1, "Laptop",
1200.00));

        products.add(new Product(2, "Keyboard",
75.00));

    }



    @GetMapping

    public ResponseEntity<List<Product>>
getAllProducts() {

        return ResponseEntity.ok(products); //
Returns 200 OK with the list of products

    }



    @GetMapping("/{id}")

    public ResponseEntity<Product>
getProductById(@PathVariable int id) {

        Optional<Product> product =
products.stream().filter(p -> p.getId() ==
id).findFirst();

        if (product.isPresent()) {

            return
ResponseEntity.ok(product.get()); // Returns 200
OK with the product
```

```java
        } else {

            return
ResponseEntity.notFound().build(); // Returns 404
Not Found

        }

    }


    @PostMapping

    public ResponseEntity<Product>
createProduct(@RequestBody Product product) {

        products.add(product);

        return
ResponseEntity.status(HttpStatus.CREATED).body(pr
oduct); // Returns 201 Created with the created
product

    }


    @DeleteMapping("/{id}")

    public ResponseEntity<Void>
deleteProduct(@PathVariable int id) {

        products.removeIf(p -> p.getId() == id);

        return
ResponseEntity.noContent().build(); // Returns
204 No Content
```

```java
    }


    @GetMapping("/search")

    public ResponseEntity<List<Product>>
searchProducts(@RequestParam String query) {

        List<Product> results = new
ArrayList<>();

        for (Product product : products) {

            if
(product.getName().toLowerCase().contains(query.t
oLowerCase())) {

                results.add(product);

            }

        }

        if (results.isEmpty()) {

            return
ResponseEntity.status(HttpStatus.NOT_FOUND).body(
new ArrayList<>()); // Returns 404 Not Found if
no results

        } else {

            return ResponseEntity.ok(results); //
Returns 200 OK with the search results

        }

    }
```

```java
}

class Product {

    private int id;

    private String name;

    private double price;


    // Constructors, getters, and setters

    public Product() {}


    public Product(int id, String name, double
price) {

        this.id = id;

        this.name = name;

        this.price = price;

    }


    public int getId() {

        return id;

    }
```

```java
    public void setId(int id) {

        this.id = id;

    }


    public String getName() {

        return name;

    }


    public void setName(String name) {

        this.name = name;

    }


    public double getPrice() {

        return price;

    }


    public void setPrice(double price) {

        this.price = price;

    }

}
```

In this example:

- ResponseEntity.ok(products): Creates a ResponseEntity with a status code of 200 OK and the list of products as the response body.
- ResponseEntity.notFound().build(): Creates a ResponseEntity with a status code of 404 Not Found and an empty response body.
- ResponseEntity.status(HttpStatus.CREATED).body(produc t): Creates a ResponseEntity with a status code of 201 Created and the created product as the response body.
- ResponseEntity.noContent().build(): Creates a ResponseEntity with a status code of 204 No Content and an empty response body.

Error Handling

Proper error handling is just as important as returning success responses. You should provide informative error messages to the client to help them understand what went wrong and how to fix it.

Spring MVC provides a few ways to handle errors:

- @ExceptionHandler: This annotation allows you to define methods that handle specific types of exceptions.

```Java
import org.springframework.http.HttpStatus;

import org.springframework.http.ResponseEntity;

import
org.springframework.web.bind.annotation.Controlle
rAdvice;
```

```java
import
org.springframework.web.bind.annotation.Exception
Handler;

import
org.springframework.web.server.ResponseStatusExce
ption;



@ControllerAdvice

public class GlobalExceptionHandler {



@ExceptionHandler(ProductNotFoundException.class)

    public ResponseEntity<String>
handleProductNotFound(ProductNotFoundException
ex) {

        return new
ResponseEntity<>(ex.getMessage(),
HttpStatus.NOT_FOUND);

    }



@ExceptionHandler(IllegalArgumentException.class)

    public ResponseEntity<String>
handleBadRequest(IllegalArgumentException ex) {
```

```java
        return new
ResponseEntity<>(ex.getMessage(),
HttpStatus.BAD_REQUEST);

    }




@ExceptionHandler(ResponseStatusException.class)

    public ResponseEntity<String>
handleResponseStatusException(ResponseStatusExcep
tion ex) {

        return new
ResponseEntity<>(ex.getReason(),
ex.getStatusCode());

    }

}




class ProductNotFoundException extends
RuntimeException {

    public ProductNotFoundException(String
message) {

        super(message);

    }

}
```

- ○ @ControllerAdvice: This annotation makes this class a global exception handler, meaning it can handle exceptions thrown by any controller.
- ○ @ExceptionHandler(ProductNotFoundException.class): This annotation specifies that the handleProductNotFound() method should handle ProductNotFoundException exceptions.
- ○ ResponseStatusException: This exception allows you to specify both a status code and a reason.
- @ResponseStatus: This annotation can be used on custom exception classes to automatically set the HTTP status code when that exception is thrown.

import org.springframework.http.HttpStatus;

import org.springframework.web.bind.annotation.ResponseStatus;

@ResponseStatus(HttpStatus.NOT_FOUND)

public class ProductNotFoundException extends RuntimeException {

public ProductNotFoundException(String message) {

super(message);

}

}

` ` `

A real-world example:

In an e-commerce API, you would use 404 Not Found when a client requests a product that doesn't exist, 400 Bad Request when the client provides invalid data for creating a product, and 500 Internal Server Error for unexpected server-side errors.

Here's a practical exercise:

1. Create a Spring MVC REST API with a few endpoints.
2. Use ResponseEntity to return different HTTP status codes for success and error scenarios.
3. Implement custom exceptions and use @ExceptionHandler or @ResponseStatus to handle them.
4. Test your API with a tool like Postman or curl to verify that the correct status codes and error messages are returned.

This exercise will give you a solid understanding of how to handle HTTP status codes and errors effectively in your Spring MVC REST APIs.

7.4 Securing RESTful APIs

Okay, let's talk about securing RESTful APIs, which is absolutely critical for protecting your data and ensuring only authorized access. Security is not an afterthought; it should be a core concern from the beginning of your API design.

So, what does securing a RESTful API involve?

At a high level, it boils down to two main concepts:

- Authentication: Verifying the identity of the client (user or application) making the request. It's about answering the question, "Who are you?"
- Authorization: Determining what resources the authenticated client is allowed to access and what actions

they are permitted to perform. It's about answering the question, "What are you allowed to do?"

Spring Security is the powerful and highly customizable framework in Spring that provides comprehensive security features. It's the standard solution for securing Spring applications, including RESTful APIs.

Here's a breakdown of common security measures and how Spring Security can help:

Authentication

There are several authentication methods you can use for REST APIs:

- Basic Authentication: This is a simple authentication scheme where the client sends the username and password in the Authorization header, encoded in Base64. While easy to implement, it's not very secure over non-HTTPS connections because the credentials are sent in plain text (after Base64 encoding, which is easily decoded).
  - Spring Security supports Basic Authentication, but it's generally recommended only for testing or internal APIs over secure connections.
- API Keys: Clients are assigned unique keys that they include in their requests (e.g., in a header or query parameter). This is a bit more secure than Basic Authentication but can still be vulnerable if the keys are compromised.
  - Spring Security can be customized to handle API keys, but you'll need to write some custom code to validate the keys.
- OAuth 2.0: This is a more robust and widely used authorization framework. It allows third-party applications to obtain limited access to resources on behalf of a user without requiring the user's credentials. It involves concepts like access tokens, refresh tokens, and different grant types.

○ Spring Security has excellent support for OAuth 2.0 through the Spring Security OAuth2 project. You can use it to implement various OAuth 2.0 flows.
- JWT (JSON Web Token): This is a popular standard for securely transmitting information between parties as a JSON object. JWTs are often used for authentication and authorization[1] in REST APIs. The server generates a JWT after successful authentication and sends it to the client. The client then includes the JWT in subsequent requests, and the server verifies its authenticity.
  ○ Spring Security can be configured to validate JWTs.

Authorization

Once a client is authenticated, you need to determine what they are allowed to do. This is where authorization comes in.

Spring Security provides mechanisms to define authorization rules based on:

- Roles: You can assign roles to users (e.g., "ADMIN," "USER," "EDITOR") and then restrict access to certain resources or methods based on these roles.
- Permissions: You can define more fine-grained permissions (e.g., "READ_PRODUCT," "WRITE_PRODUCT") and assign them to users or roles.

Spring Security Configuration for REST APIs

Spring Security is highly configurable, and you'll typically use Java configuration to define your security rules.

Here's a simplified example of configuring Spring Security for a REST API using JWT for authentication and role-based authorization:

Java

```java
import
org.springframework.context.annotation.Bean;

import
org.springframework.context.annotation.Configurat
ion;

import
org.springframework.security.config.annotation.we
b.builders.HttpSecurity;

import
org.springframework.security.config.annotation.we
b.configuration.EnableWebSecurity;

import
org.springframework.security.config.http.SessionC
reationPolicy;

import
org.springframework.security.web.SecurityFilterCh
ain;

import
org.springframework.security.web.authentication.U
sernamePasswordAuthenticationFilter;


@Configuration

@EnableWebSecurity

public class SecurityConfig {
```

```java
    private final JwtRequestFilter
jwtRequestFilter;


    public SecurityConfig(JwtRequestFilter
jwtRequestFilter) {

        this.jwtRequestFilter = jwtRequestFilter;

    }


    @Bean

    public SecurityFilterChain
securityFilterChain(HttpSecurity http) throws
Exception {

        http

            .csrf().disable() // Disable CSRF
protection (not needed for stateless REST APIs)

            .authorizeHttpRequests()


.requestMatchers("/public/**").permitAll() //
Allow access to public endpoints


.requestMatchers("/admin/**").hasRole("ADMIN") //
Require ADMIN role for /admin/**

                .anyRequest().authenticated() //
Require authentication for any other request

                .and()
```

```
        .sessionManagement()

.sessionCreationPolicy(SessionCreationPolicy.STAT
ELESS) // Don't create sessions (REST APIs are
stateless)

            .and()

        .addFilterBefore(jwtRequestFilter,
UsernamePasswordAuthenticationFilter.class); //
Add JWT filter


        return http.build();

    }

}
```

- @Configuration and @EnableWebSecurity: These annotations enable Spring Security's web security features.
- JwtRequestFilter: This is a custom filter that we would create to validate JWTs in incoming requests. It would extract the JWT from the Authorization header, verify its signature and expiration, and set the user's authentication context.
- http.csrf().disable(): CSRF (Cross-Site Request Forgery) protection is typically not needed for stateless REST APIs.
- authorizeHttpRequests(): This is where we define authorization rules.
  - requestMatchers("/public/**").permitAll(): Allows access to any URL starting with /public/ without authentication.

- o requestMatchers("/admin/**").hasRole("ADMIN"): Requires the user to have the "ADMIN" role to access any URL starting with /admin/.
- o anyRequest().authenticated(): Requires authentication for any other URL.
- sessionManagement().sessionCreationPolicy(SessionCreationPolicy.STATELESS): This tells Spring Security not to create HTTP sessions. REST APIs are typically stateless, meaning each request is independent of previous requests.
- addFilterBefore(jwtRequestFilter, UsernamePasswordAuthenticationFilter.class): This adds our custom JwtRequestFilter before Spring Security's built-in UsernamePasswordAuthenticationFilter. This ensures that our JWT validation happens before traditional username/password authentication.

Real-World Example

Consider an API for a social media application. You might have endpoints for:

- Retrieving user profiles.
- Creating posts.
- Following other users.

You would want to:

- Require authentication for all of these endpoints.
- Allow only authenticated users to create posts.
- Allow users to only access their own profile data.
- Potentially have different roles (e.g., "ADMIN," "MODERATOR") with different permissions.

Spring Security can help you implement these security rules effectively.

Practical Exercise

1. Set up a Spring Boot project and add the Spring Security dependency.
2. Implement a simple authentication mechanism (e.g., in-memory user details or a basic JWT implementation).
3. Configure Spring Security to require authentication for all API endpoints.
4. Define different roles and permissions.
5. Use Spring Security's authorization features to restrict access to certain endpoints based on roles or permissions.
6. Test your API with a tool like Postman, ensuring that unauthorized requests are rejected and authorized requests are allowed.

This exercise will give you a practical understanding of how to secure RESTful APIs using Spring Security.

Chapter 8: Spring Testing

So, what are we going to cover in this chapter? We'll explore different types of testing and how Spring provides tools to make testing easier.

8.1 Writing Unit Tests with JUnit and Mockito

Okay, let's talk in detail about unit testing, a cornerstone of software development. It's about ensuring the individual building blocks of your application work as expected. We'll explore JUnit and Mockito, two powerful tools that make unit testing in Java effective and manageable.

So, at its core, what is a unit test? It's a test that verifies the behavior of a single "unit" of code in isolation. Now, what do we mean by "unit"? Typically, a unit is the smallest testable part of your code, which is usually a method or a class. The key idea is to test this method or class without relying on any of its dependencies.

Think of it like testing the individual parts of an engine. You'd test the spark plug, the piston, and the carburetor separately to make sure each one functions correctly before you put them all together. In software, this means testing individual functions or classes to ensure they behave as designed, independent of other parts of the system.

JUnit: The Foundation

JUnit is the most widely used unit testing framework for Java. It provides the structure and tools you need to write and execute your tests. Let's break down its essential components:

- @Test Annotation: This annotation is your primary tool for defining a test. Any method annotated with @Test is recognized by JUnit as a test method and will be executed when you run your tests.

Java

```java
import org.junit.jupiter.api.Test;

class StringUtilsTest {

    @Test
    void testReverseString() {

        // Test logic here

    }


    @Test
    void testIsPalindrome() {

        // Test logic here

    }

}
```

- Assertions: Assertions are methods provided by JUnit that allow you to verify expected outcomes. They are like checks that you place within your test to confirm that the code under test behaves as you anticipate. If an assertion fails, the test is considered failed.

Here are some of the most commonly used JUnit assertions:

- o assertEquals(expected, actual): This assertion is used to check if the actual value is equal to the expected value. It's used for comparing numbers, strings, objects, etc.

Java

```java
import org.junit.jupiter.api.Test;

import static
org.junit.jupiter.api.Assertions.assertEquals;


class CalculatorTest {

    @Test

    void testAdd() {

        Calculator calculator = new Calculator();

        int result = calculator.add(5, 3);

        assertEquals(8, result);
```

```java
        }

}


class Calculator {

    int add(int a, int b) {

        return a + b;

    }

}
```

- ○ assertTrue(condition): This assertion checks if the given condition is true.

Java

```java
import org.junit.jupiter.api.Test;

import static
org.junit.jupiter.api.Assertions.assertTrue;


class ValidationTest {

    @Test

    void testIsEmailValid() {
```

```java
        Validation validation = new Validation();

assertTrue(validation.isEmailValid("test@example.
com"));

    }

}


class Validation {

    boolean isEmailValid(String email) {

        return email.contains("@") &&
email.contains(".");

    }

}
```

   o assertFalse(condition): This assertion checks if the
      given condition is false.

Java

```java
import org.junit.jupiter.api.Test;

import static
org.junit.jupiter.api.Assertions.assertFalse;


class ValidationTest {
```

```java
@Test

void testIsEmailInvalid() {

    Validation validation = new Validation();

assertFalse(validation.isEmailValid("invalid-emai
l"));

    }

}


class Validation {

    boolean isEmailValid(String email) {

        return email.contains("@") &&
email.contains(".");

    }

}
```

   ○ assertNotNull(object): This assertion checks if the
     given object is not null.

Java

```java
import org.junit.jupiter.api.Test;
```

```java
import static
org.junit.jupiter.api.Assertions.assertNotNull;


class DataFetcherTest {


    @Test

    void testFetchData() {

        DataFetcher fetcher = new DataFetcher();

        String data = fetcher.fetchData();

        assertNotNull(data);

    }

}


class DataFetcher {

    String fetchData() {

        return "Some data";

    }

}
```

  o assertNull(object): This assertion checks if the given
     object is null.

Java

```java
import org.junit.jupiter.api.Test;

import static
org.junit.jupiter.api.Assertions.assertNull;


class DataFetcherTest {

    @Test

    void testFetchNullData() {

        DataFetcher fetcher = new DataFetcher();

        String data = fetcher.fetchNullData();

        assertNull(data);

    }

}


class DataFetcher {

    String fetchNullData() {

        return null;

    }

}
```

- assertThrows(expectedType, executable): This assertion verifies that the given executable code throws an exception of the expectedType.

Java

```java
import org.junit.jupiter.api.Test;

import static
org.junit.jupiter.api.Assertions.assertThrows;


class CalculatorTest {

    @Test

    void testDivideByZero() {

        Calculator calculator = new Calculator();

        assertThrows(ArithmeticException.class,
() -> calculator.divide(10, 0));

    }

}


class Calculator {

    int divide(int a, int b) {
```

```
        if (b == 0) {

            throw new ArithmeticException("Cannot
divide by zero");

        }

        return a / b;

    }

}
```

- Test Lifecycle Annotations: JUnit provides annotations to control the setup and teardown of your tests, allowing you to execute code before or after test methods.
  - @BeforeEach: This annotation marks a method to be executed before *each* test method in the class. It's useful for initializing objects or setting up test data that will be used by multiple tests.

import org.junit.jupiter.api.BeforeEach;

import org.junit.jupiter.api.Test;

import static org.junit.jupiter.api.Assertions.assertEquals;1

class StringProcessorTest {

private StringProcessor processor;

@BeforeEach

```java
void setUp() {

    processor = new StringProcessor();

}


@Test

void testToUpper() {

    String result = processor.toUpper("hello");

    assertEquals("HELLO", result);

}


@Test

void testTrim() {

    String result = processor.trim(" test ");

    assertEquals("test", result);

}
}


class StringProcessor {

    String toUpper(String str) {

        return str.toUpperCase();
```

```java
    }

    String trim(String str) {

        return str.trim();

    }

}
```

`@AfterEach`: This annotation marks a method to be executed after each test method in the class. It's useful for cleaning up resources or resetting the state after a test.

```java
import org.junit.jupiter.api.AfterEach;

import org.junit.jupiter.api.BeforeEach;

import org.junit.jupiter.api.Test;

import static org.junit.jupiter.api.Assertions.assertEquals;


class StringProcessorTest {


    private StringProcessor processor;
```

```java
    @BeforeEach

    void setUp() {

        processor = new StringProcessor();

    }


    @AfterEach

    void tearDown() {

        processor = null; // Example: Releasing resources
(not strictly necessary here)

    }


    @Test

    void testToUpper() {

        String result = processor.toUpper("hello");

        assertEquals("HELLO", result);

    }


    @Test

    void testTrim() {

        String result = processor.trim(" test ");
```

```java
    assertEquals("test", result);

  }

}


class StringProcessor {

  String toUpper(String str) {

    return str.toUpperCase();

  }


  String trim(String str) {

    return str.trim();

  }

}
```

`@BeforeAll`: This annotation marks a static method to be executed once before all test methods in the class. It's useful for expensive setup operations that only need to be performed once.

```java
import org.junit.jupiter.api.BeforeAll;

import org.junit.jupiter.api.Test;
```

```java
import static
org.junit.jupiter.api.Assertions.assertEquals;


class DatabaseConnectionTest {


    private static DatabaseConnection connection;


    @BeforeAll
    static void setUpAll() {
        connection = new DatabaseConnection();
        connection.connect(); // Establish connection (expensive operation)
    }


    @Test
    void testQuery() {
        String result = connection.executeQuery("SELECT * FROM users");
        assertEquals("User Data", result);
    }


    // Other test methods...
```

```java
}

class DatabaseConnection {

    void connect() {}

    String executeQuery(String query) { return "User Data"; }

}
```

`@AfterAll`: This annotation marks a static method to be executed once after all test methods in the class. It's useful for expensive cleanup operations that only need to be performed once.

```java
import org.junit.jupiter.api.AfterAll;

import org.junit.jupiter.api.BeforeAll;

import org.junit.jupiter.api.Test;

import static org.junit.jupiter.api.Assertions.assertEquals;

class DatabaseConnectionTest {

    private static DatabaseConnection connection;
```

```java
@BeforeAll
static void setUpAll() {

    connection = new DatabaseConnection();

    connection.connect(); // Establish connection
(expensive operation)

}


@AfterAll
static void tearDownAll() {

    connection.disconnect(); // Close connection
(expensive operation)

}


@Test
void testQuery() {

    String result = connection.executeQuery("SELECT
* FROM users");

    assertEquals("User Data", result);

}


// Other test methods...
```

```
    }


    class DatabaseConnection {

        void connect() {}

        void disconnect() {}

        String executeQuery(String query) { return "User
Data"; }

    }

    ` ` `
```

Mockito: Mocking Dependencies

Now, let's talk about Mockito. In real-world applications, classes often depend on other classes. You don't want to test the dependencies; you want to isolate the class you're testing. That's where mocking comes in.

Mockito is a mocking framework that allows you to create "mock" objects. Mock objects are fake objects that simulate the behavior of real objects.

You can use them to:

- Replace dependencies: Provide controlled inputs to the class you're testing without actually using the real dependencies.
- Verify interactions: Check if the class you're testing calls the dependency methods as expected.

Here are the key Mockito features:

- Mockito.mock(Class): This method creates a mock object of the specified class or interface.

Java

```java
import org.mockito.Mockito;


interface MessageService {

    String sendMessage(String recipient, String
message);

}


class MessageSender {

    private MessageService service;


    MessageSender(MessageService service) {

        this.service = service;

    }


    void send(String recipient, String message) {

        service.sendMessage(recipient, message);

    }

}
```

```java
class MessageSenderTest {


    @Test

    void testSendMessage() {

        MessageService mockService =
Mockito.mock(MessageService.class);

        MessageSender sender = new
MessageSender(mockService);

        // ...

    }

}
```

- Mockito.when(mock.method(args)).thenReturn(value):
  This method configures the mock object to return a specific
  value when a method is called with the specified args.

Java

```java
import org.mockito.Mockito;

import org.junit.jupiter.api.Test;

import static
org.junit.jupiter.api.Assertions.assertEquals;


interface MessageService {
```

```java
    String sendMessage(String recipient, String
message);

}


class MessageSender {

    private MessageService service;


    MessageSender(MessageService service) {

        this.service = service;

    }


    String send(String recipient, String message)
{

        return service.sendMessage("John",
"Hello!");

    }

}


class MessageSenderTest {

    @Test

    void testSendMessage() {
```

```java
    MessageService mockService =
Mockito.mock(MessageService.class);


Mockito.when(mockService.sendMessage("John",
"Hello!")).thenReturn("Message Sent!");



    MessageSender sender = new
MessageSender(mockService);

    String result = sender.send("John",
"Hello!");

    assertEquals("Message Sent!", result);

  }

}
```

- Mockito.verify(mock).method(args): This method verifies that a method on the mock object was called with the specified args.

Java

```java
import org.mockito.Mockito;

import org.junit.jupiter.api.Test;

import static
org.junit.jupiter.api.Assertions.assertEquals;



interface MessageService {
```

```java
    String sendMessage(String recipient, String
message);

}


class MessageSender {

    private MessageService service;


    MessageSender(MessageService service) {

        this.service = service;

    }


    String send(String recipient, String message)
{

        return service.sendMessage("John",
"Hello!");

    }

}


class MessageSenderTest {

    @Test

    void testSendMessage() {
```

```
        MessageService mockService =
Mockito.mock(MessageService.class);


Mockito.when(mockService.sendMessage("John",
"Hello!")).thenReturn("Message Sent!");



        MessageSender sender = new
MessageSender(mockService);

        String result = sender.send("John",
"Hello!");

        assertEquals("Message Sent!", result);


Mockito.verify(mockService).sendMessage("John",
"Hello!"); // Verify sendMessage was called

    }

}
```

Real-World Example

Consider a service that processes orders. This service might depend on a PaymentGateway to handle payments and a NotificationService to send confirmation emails. In unit tests, you would mock the PaymentGateway and NotificationService to control their behavior and verify that the order service interacts with them correctly, without actually making real payment transactions or sending emails.

Practical Exercise

1. Choose a simple class you've written recently.
2. Write a set of unit tests for its methods using JUnit.

3. If the class has any dependencies on other classes or interfaces, use Mockito to create mock objects for those dependencies.
4. Experiment with different JUnit assertions and Mockito's mocking and verification capabilities.

This exercise will give you a hands-on experience with unit testing and help you solidify your understanding of JUnit and Mockito, which are essential tools for any Java developer.

8.2 Integration Testing with Spring Test

Okay, let's move beyond unit testing and talk about integration testing. While unit tests focus on individual components in isolation, integration tests verify how different parts of your application work together. This is a crucial step to ensure that your application functions correctly as a whole. Spring Test provides a suite of tools to make integration testing Spring applications much easier.

So, what exactly *is* integration testing? It's about testing the interactions between different modules or components of your application. This might involve testing:

- Interactions between different classes or services within your application.
- Interactions with external systems like databases, message queues, or web services.
- The overall flow of a specific use case or feature.

Think of it like testing the engine, transmission, and wheels of a car together. You've already tested each part individually (unit tests), but now you want to make sure they work seamlessly as a system.

Spring Test offers several key features to help you with integration testing:

- Application Context Loading: One of the core features is the ability to load a Spring ApplicationContext within your tests. This means you can have Spring create and wire up your beans, just like it does in a running application. This is incredibly useful for testing components that rely on Spring's Dependency Injection.
  - @SpringBootTest: This annotation is commonly used in Spring Boot applications. It tells Spring Boot to load the full application context, including all your beans and configurations. It's suitable for testing how your application works in a production-like environment.

import org.junit.jupiter.api.Test;

import org.springframework.beans.factory.annotation.Autowired;

import org.springframework.boot.test.context.SpringBootTest;1

import static org.junit.jupiter.api.Assertions.*;

@SpringBootTest

class MyServiceIntegrationTest {

@Autowired

private MyService myService;

```java
    @Test

    void testGetData() {

        String data = myService.getData();

        assertNotNull(data);

        assertEquals("Some data", data);

    }

}


import org.springframework.stereotype.Service;


@Service

class MyService {


    String getData() {

        return "Some data";

    }

}
```

In this example, `@SpringBootTest` loads the entire application context, and `@Autowired` injects the `MyService` bean into the test class.

`@ContextConfiguration`: This annotation allows you to load a specific configuration for your tests. You can use it to load only the necessary beans and avoid loading the entire application context, which can be faster for some tests.

```java
import org.junit.jupiter.api.Test;

import org.springframework.beans.factory.annotation.Autowired;

import org.springframework.test.context.ContextConfiguration;
2

import org.springframework.test.context.junit.jupiter.SpringJUnitConfig;3

import static org.junit.jupiter.api.Assertions.*;

@SpringJUnitConfig

@ContextConfiguration(classes = {MyServiceConfig.class})

class MyServiceIntegrationTest {


    @Autowired
```

```java
    private MyService myService;

    @Test
    void testGetData() {
        String data = myService.getData();
        assertNotNull(data);
        assertEquals("Some data", data);
    }
}


import org.springframework.context.annotation.Bean;
import org.springframework.context.annotation.Configuration;


@Configuration
class MyServiceConfig {

    @Bean
    MyServicc myService() {
        return new MyService();
    }
```

```
}


import org.springframework.stereotype.Service;


@Service

class MyService {


    String getData() {

        return "Some data";

    }

}
```
```

Here, `@ContextConfiguration` is used to load a specific configuration class (`MyServiceConfig`) that defines the `MyService` bean.

- Transaction Management: Spring Test provides support for managing transactions in your tests. You can use annotations like @Transactional to automatically roll back any database changes made during a test, ensuring that your test data remains clean.
    - @Transactional: This annotation, when used in a test class, automatically rolls back the transaction after each test method.
```

```java
import org.junit.jupiter.api.Test;

import org.springframework.beans.factory.annotation.Autowired;

import org.springframework.boot.test.context.SpringBootTest;4

import org.springframework.transaction.annotation.Transactional;5

import static org.junit.jupiter.api.Assertions.*;

  @SpringBootTest

  @Transactional

  class MyServiceDatabaseTest {


    @Autowired

    private MyService myService;


    @Test

    void testSaveAndRetrieveData() {

      String initialData = "Test Data";

      myService.saveData(initialData);


      String retrievedData = myService.retrieveData();
```

```
        assertEquals(initialData, retrievedData);

    }

}


import org.springframework.stereotype.Service;


@Service
class MyService {

    private String data;

    void saveData(String data) {
        this.data = data;
    }


    String retrieveData() {
        return data;
    }
}
```
```
```

- Mocking and Stubbing: While Mockito is primarily used for unit testing, Spring Test also provides some support for mocking and stubbing, especially when dealing with external dependencies. However, for complex mocking scenarios, it's often best to combine Spring Test with Mockito.

Real-World Example

Consider an e-commerce application. An integration test might verify the following scenario:

1. A user adds items to their shopping cart.
2. The user proceeds to checkout.
3. The payment service is called to process the payment.
4. The order is saved to the database.
5. A confirmation email is sent to the user.

This test would involve multiple components (e.g., shopping cart service, payment service, order service, email service, database access) and would verify that they all work together correctly.

Practical Exercise

1. Create a Spring Boot application with a few interconnected services.
2. Write integration tests that verify the interactions between these services.
3. Use @SpringBootTest or @ContextConfiguration to load the application context.
4. Experiment with @Transactional to manage database transactions during your tests.
5. (Optional) Introduce a simulated failure in one of the services and verify that the system handles it correctly.

This exercise will provide you with valuable experience in writing integration tests for Spring applications, helping you build more robust and reliable software.

8.3 Testing Spring MVC Controllers and RESTful APIs

Okay, let's focus on how to test Spring MVC controllers and RESTful APIs effectively. This is a crucial aspect of ensuring your web applications and APIs function correctly, especially when dealing with HTTP requests and responses.

Testing controllers and APIs is a bit different from testing plain Java classes. You need to simulate HTTP requests and verify that your controllers handle them correctly, produce the expected responses, and interact with other components as intended.

Spring Test provides a powerful tool called MockMvc specifically for this purpose.

MockMvc: **Simulating HTTP Requests**

MockMvc allows you to test your Spring MVC controllers without starting a full-fledged web server. It simulates the behavior of a web server, enabling you to send requests and verify responses in a controlled environment.

Here's how MockMvc works:

1. Setting up MockMvc: You can set up MockMvc in your test class using annotations or programmatically.
   - @AutoConfigureMockMvc (Spring Boot): This annotation is a convenient way to automatically configure MockMvc in a Spring Boot test. It's typically used with @SpringBootTest to load the application context.

```java
import org.junit.jupiter.api.Test;

import
org.springframework.beans.factory.annotation.Autowired;

import
org.springframework.boot.test.autoconfigure.web.servlet.AutoConfigureMockMvc;1

import
org.springframework.boot.test.context.SpringBootTest;

import org.springframework.test.web.servlet.MockMvc;

import
org.springframework.test.web.servlet.request.MockMvcRequestBuilders;

import
org.springframework.test.web.servlet.result.MockMvcResultMatchers;2

  @SpringBootTest

  @AutoConfigureMockMvc

  class GreetingControllerWebTest {


    @Autowired

    private MockMvc mockMvc;


    @Test
```

```java
void testGreetingEndpoint() throws Exception {

mockMvc.perform(MockMvcRequestBuilders.get("/greeting").param("name", "World"))

.andExpect(MockMvcResultMatchers.status().isOk())

.andExpect(MockMvcResultMatchers.content().string("Hello, World!"));
    }
  }


    import org.springframework.stereotype.Controller;

    import org.springframework.web.bind.annotation.GetMapping;

    import org.springframework.web.bind.annotation.RequestParam;

    import org.springframework.web.bind.annotation.ResponseBody;


    @Controller

    class GreetingController {
```

```java
@GetMapping("/greeting")

@ResponseBody

String greeting(@RequestParam String name) {

    return "Hello, " + name + "!";

  }

}

```
```

`@WebMvcTest` (Spring Boot): This annotation is used to test only a specific Spring MVC controller. It loads only the necessary Spring beans for that controller, which can make your tests faster.

```java
import org.junit.jupiter.api.Test;

import org.springframework.beans.factory.annotation.Autowired;

import org.springframework.boot.test.autoconfigure.web.servlet.WebMvcTest;3

import org.springframework.test.web.servlet.MockMvc;
```
```

```java
import4
org.springframework.test.web.servlet.request.MockMvc
RequestBuilders;

import
org.springframework.test.web.servlet.result.MockMvcRe
sultMatchers;5

@WebMvcTest(GreetingController.class)

class GreetingControllerWebTest {


    @Autowired

    private MockMvc mockMvc;


    @Test

    void testGreetingEndpoint() throws Exception {

mockMvc.perform(MockMvcRequestBuilders.get("/greet
ing").param("name", "World"))

.andExpect(MockMvcResultMatchers.status().isOk())

.andExpect(MockMvcResultMatchers.content().string("
Hello, World!"));

    }

  }
```

```java
import org.springframework.stereotype.Controller;

import org.springframework.web.bind.annotation.GetMapping;

import org.springframework.web.bind.annotation.RequestParam;

import org.springframework.web.bind.annotation.ResponseBody;


@Controller
class GreetingController {


  @GetMapping("/greeting")
  @ResponseBody
  String greeting(@RequestParam String name) {
    return "Hello, " + name + "!";
  }
}
```

Programmatic Setup: You can also set up `MockMvc` programmatically, which gives you more control but requires more code.

2. Performing Requests: You use MockMvc.perform() to simulate an HTTP request. You can specify the HTTP method (GET, POST, PUT, DELETE), the URL, request parameters, headers, and request body.
   - MockMvcRequestBuilders: This class provides static methods to build MockHttpServletRequest objects, which represent HTTP requests.

Java

```
mockMvc.perform(MockMvcRequestBuilders.get("/gree
ting").param("name", "World"))
```

   - This code simulates a GET request to the /greeting URL with a request parameter named "name" and the value "World".

3. Verifying Responses: You use MockMvcResultMatchers to make assertions about the response. You can verify the status code, headers, content, and other aspects of the response.
   - MockMvcResultMatchers: This class provides static methods to create ResultMatcher objects, which are used to make assertions about the response.

Java

```
.andExpect(MockMvcResultMatchers.status().isOk())

.andExpect(MockMvcResultMatchers.content().string
("Hello, World!"))
```

  - This code checks that the response status code is 200 OK and that the response content is the string "Hello, World!".

Examples

Let's look at some more detailed examples:

Testing a REST API endpoint that returns JSON:

import org.junit.jupiter.api.Test;

import org.springframework.beans.factory.annotation.Autowired;

import org.springframework.boot.test.autoconfigure.web.servlet.AutoConfigureMockMvc;6

import org.springframework.boot.test.context.SpringBootTest;

import org.springframework.http.MediaType;

import org.springframework.test.web.servlet.MockMvc;

import org.springframework.test.web.servlet.request.MockMvcRequestBuilders;7

```java
import
org.springframework.test.web.servlet.result.MockMvcResultMatchers;8

@SpringBootTest

@AutoConfigureMockMvc

class ProductControllerWebTest {


    @Autowired

    private MockMvc mockMvc;


    @Test

    void testGetProductById() throws Exception {

mockMvc.perform(MockMvcRequestBuilders.get("/products/1"))

.andExpect(MockMvcResultMatchers.status().isOk())

.andExpect(MockMvcResultMatchers.content().contentType(MediaType.APPLICATION_JSON))

.andExpect(MockMvcResultMatchers.jsonPath("$.id").value(1))
```

```java
                    .andExpect(MockMvcResultMatchers.jsonPath("$.name"
).value("Laptop"));

    }

}


import org.springframework.web.bind.annotation.*;

import java.util.ArrayList;

import java.util.List;


@RestController

@RequestMapping("/products")

class ProductController {


    private final List<Product> products = new
ArrayList<>();


    public ProductController() {

        products.add(new Product(1, "Laptop", 1200.00));

        products.add(new Product(2, "Keyboard", 75.00));

    }
```

```java
    @GetMapping("/{id}")
    public Product getProductById(@PathVariable int id) {
        for (Product product : products) {
            if (product.getId() == id) {
                return product;
            }
        }
        return null;
    }
}


class Product {
    private int id;
    private String name;
    private double price;

    public Product(int id, String name, double price) {
        this.id = id;
        this.name = name;
        this.price = price;
```

```java
    }

    public int getId() {
        return id;
    }

    public void setId(int id) {
        this.id = id;
    }

    public String getName() {
        return name;
    }

    public void setName(String name) {
        this.name = name;
    }

    public double getPrice() {
        return price;
```

```
    }


    public void setPrice(double price) {

       this.price = price;

    }

}

```
```

*
`MockMvcResultMatchers.content().contentType(Media
Type.APPLICATION_JSON)`: This checks that the
response content type is `application/json`.

 `MockMvcResultMatchers.jsonPath("$.id").value(1)`:
This uses JsonPath to navigate the JSON response and
check that the "id" field has the value 1.

Testing a POST request with JSON data:

import org.junit.jupiter.api.Test;

**import
org.springframework.beans.factory.annotation.Autowire
d;**

**import
org.springframework.boot.test.autoconfigure.web.servle
t.AutoConfigureMockMvc;9**
```

```java
import
org.springframework.boot.test.context.SpringBootTest;

import org.springframework.http.MediaType;

import org.springframework.test.web.servlet.MockMvc;

import
org.springframework.test.web.servlet.request.MockMvc
RequestBuilders;10

import
org.springframework.test.web.servlet.result.MockMvcRe
sultMatchers;11

@SpringBootTest

@AutoConfigureMockMvc

class ProductControllerWebTest {


    @Autowired

    private MockMvc mockMvc;


    @Test

    void testCreateProduct() throws Exception {

        String productJson =
"{\"name\":\"Mouse\",\"price\":25.00}";
```

```
mockMvc.perform(MockMvcRequestBuilders.post("/pro
ducts")

.contentType(MediaType.APPLICATION_JSON)

        .content(productJson))

.andExpect(MockMvcResultMatchers.status().isCreated(
))

.andExpect(MockMvcResultMatchers.jsonPath("$.name"
).value("Mouse"));

    }

}


import org.springframework.web.bind.annotation.*;

import org.springframework.http.HttpStatus;

import org.springframework.http.ResponseEntity;

import java.util.ArrayList;

import java.util.List;


@RestController

@RequestMapping("/products")
```

```java
class ProductController {

    private final List<Product> products = new ArrayList<>();

    private int nextId = 3;


    @PostMapping
    public ResponseEntity<Product>
createProduct(@RequestBody Product product) {

        product.setId(nextId++);

        products.add(product);

        return
ResponseEntity.status(HttpStatus.CREATED).body(product);

    }
}


class Product {
    private int id;

    private String name;

    private double price;
```

```java
public Product() {}

public Product(int id, String name, double price) {
    this.id = id;
    this.name = name;
    this.price = price;
}

public int getId() {
    return id;
}

public void setId(int id) {
    this.id = id;
}

public String getName() {
    return name;
}
```

```java
    public void setName(String name) {

        this.name = name;

    }


    public double getPrice() {

        return price;

    }


    public void setPrice(double price) {

        this.price = price;

    }

}
```
```

`MockMvcRequestBuilders.post("/products").contentType(MediaType.APPLICATION_JSON).content(productJson)`: This simulates a POST request to `/products` with the JSON data in the request body.

* `MockMvcResultMatchers.status().isCreated()`: This checks that the response status code is 201 Created (indicating successful creation).

**Real-World Example**

Consider an API for a social media application. You would use MockMvc to test endpoints for:
```

- Creating a new post (POST /posts).
- Retrieving a list of posts (GET /posts).
- Retrieving a specific post (GET /posts/{postId}).
- Updating a post (PUT /posts/{postId}).
- Deleting a post (DELETE /posts/{postId}).

You would verify things like:

- Correct status codes (e.g., 200 OK, 201 Created, 404 Not Found).
- Correct data formats (e.g., JSON).
- Correct data in the response body.
- Security constraints (e.g., only authorized users can create posts).

Practical Exercise

1. Create a Spring MVC REST API with a few endpoints.
2. Write tests for these endpoints using MockMvc.
3. Experiment with different HTTP methods, request parameters, request headers, and request bodies.
4. Use MockMvcResultMatchers to verify various aspects of the response, including status codes, content types, and response data.
5. Practice using JsonPath to extract and verify specific values from JSON responses.

This exercise will provide you with solid experience in testing Spring MVC controllers and RESTful APIs, enabling you to build more reliable web applications and APIs.

8.4 Testing Data Access Layers

Okay, let's talk about testing data access layers in Spring applications. This is a crucial aspect of ensuring the reliability of your application's interactions with databases. Your data access layer, often implemented as DAOs (Data Access Objects) or repositories (with Spring Data JPA), is responsible for persisting and retrieving data, so testing it thoroughly is essential.

So, what are the challenges in testing data access layers?

- Database Dependency: The biggest challenge is the dependency on a real database. You don't want your tests to rely on a production database, as this can lead to data corruption and unpredictable results.
- Test Data Setup and Cleanup: You need a way to set up test data before your tests and clean it up afterward to ensure test isolation.
- Slow Tests: Interacting with a real database can be slow, making your tests run longer.

Spring provides some tools and techniques to address these challenges:

1. In-Memory Databases

A common approach is to use an in-memory database for testing. In-memory databases are databases that run in your application's memory and don't persist data to disk. They're fast, lightweight, and easy to set up.

- H2 Database: H2 is a popular open-source, in-memory database that's often used for testing Spring applications. Spring Boot simplifies its configuration.

Here's an example of using H2 with Spring Data JPA for testing:

import org.junit.jupiter.api.Test;

```java
import
org.springframework.beans.factory.annotation.Autowire
d;

import
org.springframework.boot.test.autoconfigure.orm.jpa.D
ataJpaTest;1

import org.springframework.test.context.jdbc.Sql;

import static org.junit.jupiter.api.Assertions.*;2

import javax.persistence.Entity;

import javax.persistence.GeneratedValue;

import javax.persistence.GenerationType;

import javax.persistence.Id;

import3
org.springframework.data.jpa.repository.JpaRepository;

 @DataJpaTest

 @Sql("/insert-data.sql") // Optional: Load data before
the test

 class UserRepositoryTest {


    @Autowired

    private UserRepository userRepository;


    @Test
```

```java
    void testFindById() {

        User user =
userRepository.findById(1L).orElse(null);

        assertNotNull(user);

        assertEquals("John Doe", user.getUsername());

    }


    @Test

    void testSaveUser() {

        User newUser = new User();

        newUser.setUsername("Jane Smith");

        newUser.setEmail("jane.smith@example.com");

        userRepository.save(newUser);


        User savedUser =
userRepository.findByUsername("Jane Smith");

        assertNotNull(savedUser);

        assertEquals("jane.smith@example.com",
savedUser.getEmail());

    }

}
```

```java
interface UserRepository extends JpaRepository<User,
Long> {

    User findByUsername(String username);

}


@Entity
class User {

    @Id

    @GeneratedValue(strategy =
GenerationType.IDENTITY)

    private Long id;

    private String username;

    private String email;


    // Constructors, getters, and setters
    public User() {}


    public User(Long id, String username, String email) {

        this.id = id;

        this.username = username;

        this.email = email;
```

```java
    }


    public Long getId() {

        return id;

    }


    public void setId(Long id) {

        this.id = id;

    }


    public String getUsername() {

        return username;

    }


    public void setUsername(String username) {

        this.username = username;

    }


    public String getEmail() {

        return email;
```

```
        }


    public void setEmail(String email) {

        this.email = email;

    }

}

```
```

* `@DataJpaTest`: This Spring Boot annotation is specifically designed for testing JPA components (like repositories). It configures an in-memory database (H2 by default), sets up Spring Data JPA, and automatically rolls back transactions after each test. This ensures that your tests don't pollute the database.

`@Sql("/insert-data.sql")`: This annotation (optional) allows you to execute SQL scripts to populate the database with test data before your tests run. This is useful for setting up initial conditions.

2. Transaction Management

Spring Test provides excellent transaction management support for your tests. You can use the @Transactional annotation to ensure that any database changes made during a test are automatically rolled back, leaving your database in a clean state.

- @Transactional: When applied to a test class or method, this annotation automatically rolls back the transaction after the test is completed.
```

```java
import org.junit.jupiter.api.Test;

import org.springframework.beans.factory.annotation.Autowired;

import org.springframework.boot.test.context.SpringBootTest;4

import org.springframework.transaction.annotation.Transactional;5

import static org.junit.jupiter.api.Assertions.*;

import org.springframework.stereotype.Service;6

@SpringBootTest

@Transactional

class MyServiceDatabaseTest {

    @Autowired

    private MyService myService;

    @Test

    void testSaveAndRetrieveData() {

        String initialData = "Test Data";

        myService.saveData(initialData);
```

```java
        String retrievedData = myService.retrieveData();

        assertEquals(initialData, retrievedData);
    }
}


@Service
class MyService {

    private String data;

    void saveData(String data) {
        this.data = data;
    }


    String retrieveData() {
        return data;
    }
}
```

In this example, `@Transactional` ensures that any changes made to the database by `myService.saveData()` are rolled back after the `testSaveAndRetrieveData()` method finishes.

3. Mocking and Stubbing

While in-memory databases are great for testing data access logic, you might still want to mock or stub certain database interactions or external dependencies within your data access layer. You can use Mockito or other mocking frameworks in conjunction with Spring Test for this purpose.

For example, if your data access layer interacts with a complex stored procedure, you might want to mock the stored procedure call to avoid relying on its specific behavior during your tests.

Real-World Example

Consider an e-commerce application. You would want to test your data access layer to ensure that:

- You can correctly retrieve product information from the database.
- You can save new orders and update inventory levels.
- You can handle database errors gracefully (e.g., connection failures, data validation errors).

Using an in-memory database like H2 and Spring Test's transaction management features, you can thoroughly test these scenarios without affecting your production data.

Practical Exercise

1. Set up a Spring Boot application with Spring Data JPA and a simple entity (e.g., Product, Order).
2. Create a repository interface for your entity.
3. Write tests for your repository using @DataJpaTest.
4. Use @Sql to populate the database with test data.

5. Use @Transactional to ensure test isolation.
6. Experiment with different repository methods (e.g., save(), findById(), findAll(), custom query methods).
7. (Optional) Introduce a simulated database error (e.g., by providing invalid data) and verify that your repository handles it correctly.

This exercise will give you practical experience in testing data access layers in Spring applications, helping you build more robust and reliable data persistence logic.

Chapter 9: Spring Boot Essentials

So, you're familiar with Spring, right? It's great, but sometimes it can feel like you're spending more time configuring things than actually writing code. That's where Spring Boot comes in. Spring Boot takes the pain out of Spring development by providing sensible defaults and automating much of the setup process.

9.1 Spring Boot Autoconfiguration

Okay, let's talk in detail about Spring Boot's autoconfiguration. This is one of its most powerful features, and it's what makes Spring Boot so much easier to use than traditional Spring.

So, what is autoconfiguration?

In essence, it's Spring Boot's way of automatically configuring your Spring application based on the dependencies you've added to your project. It tries to "guess" what beans you need and sets them up for you, so you don't have to write a lot of configuration code.

To understand this, let's first appreciate the traditional way Spring used to be configured. You had to explicitly define every bean (object) and its dependencies in XML files or Java configuration classes. This was very verbose and required a deep understanding of the Spring framework.

Spring Boot autoconfiguration aims to reduce this boilerplate. It examines your project's dependencies and then, based on what it finds, creates and registers beans in the Spring ApplicationContext.

Here's how it works in more detail:

1. @EnableAutoConfiguration: This annotation is the key to enabling autoconfiguration. It's typically placed on your main application class (the one with the main method).

293

Spring Boot looks for this annotation to know that it should perform autoconfiguration.

import org.springframework.boot.SpringApplication;

import org.springframework.boot.autoconfigure.SpringBootApplication;1

@SpringBootApplication // A convenience annotation that includes @EnableAutoConfiguration

public class MyApp {

    public static void main(String[] args) {

      SpringApplication.run(MyApp.class, args);

    }

}

` ` `

`@SpringBootApplication` is a convenience annotation that combines `@EnableAutoConfiguration`, `@ComponentScan`, and `@Configuration`. It's the standard annotation for Spring Boot applications.

2. ConditionalOn... Annotations: Spring Boot uses a set of @ConditionalOn... annotations to control autoconfiguration. These annotations specify conditions that must be met for a particular configuration to be applied.

For example:

- o @ConditionalOnClass(DataSource.class): This annotation means that the configuration should be applied only if the DataSource class is present on the classpath (i.e., if you've added a JDBC driver dependency).
- o @ConditionalOnMissingBean(DataSource.class): This annotation means that the configuration should be applied only if there's no bean of type DataSource already defined in the ApplicationContext.
- o @ConditionalOnProperty("spring.datasource.url"): This annotation means that the configuration should be applied only if the spring.datasource.url property is set.

3. These annotations allow Spring Boot to be very precise in what it configures.
4. spring.factories: Spring Boot uses a file called spring.factories to discover autoconfiguration classes. This file is located in the META-INF/spring.factories directory within Spring Boot's starter dependencies. It lists the classes that should be considered for autoconfiguration.
5. When Spring Boot starts, it reads these spring.factories files and evaluates the @ConditionalOn... annotations on each autoconfiguration class. If the conditions are met, the configuration class is processed, and its beans are registered in the ApplicationContext.

Examples of Autoconfiguration

Let's look at some concrete examples to understand how autoconfiguration works:

- Web Development: If you add the spring-boot-starter-web dependency, Spring Boot will automatically configure a web server (Tomcat by default), Spring MVC's DispatcherServlet, a ViewResolver (if needed), and other web-related components. You don't have to write any configuration code for these.

XML

```
<dependency>

    <groupId>org.springframework.boot</groupId>

<artifactId>spring-boot-starter-web</artifactId>

</dependency>
```

- Database Access:[2] If you add a JDBC driver dependency (e.g., for MySQL, PostgreSQL), Spring Boot will automatically configure a DataSource for you. You typically only need to provide database connection properties (URL, username, password) in your application.properties or application.yml file.

XML

```
<dependency>

    <groupId>com.mysql</groupId>

    <artifactId>mysql-connector-j</artifactId>

</dependency>
```

Properties

```
spring.datasource.url=jdbc:mysql://localhost:3306
/mydb

spring.datasource.username=user

spring.datasource.password=password
```

- JPA (Java Persistence API): If you add the spring-boot-starter-data-jpa dependency and a database driver, Spring Boot will configure JPA for you, including an EntityManagerFactory. You only need to define your JPA entities and repositories.

<dependency>

<groupId>org.springframework.boot</groupId>

<artifactId>spring-boot-starter-data-jpa</artifactId>

</dependency>

<dependency>3

<groupId>com.h2database</groupId>

<artifactId>h2</artifactId>

<scope>runtime</scope>

</dependency>4

```
```

(H2 is an in-memory database, often used for development)

Benefits of Autoconfiguration

- Reduced Boilerplate: It significantly reduces the amount of configuration code you need to write.
- Increased Productivity: You can develop applications much faster.
- Simplified Dependency Management: It helps ensure compatibility between different libraries.
- Convention over Configuration: It promotes a convention-over-configuration approach, where Spring Boot provides sensible defaults, but you can still customize them if needed.

Important Note:

While autoconfiguration is powerful, it's essential to understand that it's not "magic." Spring Boot makes educated guesses based on your dependencies. You can always override or customize the autoconfigured beans if you need more control.

Practical Exercise

1. Create a new Spring Boot project using Spring Initializr or your IDE.
2. Add different Spring Boot starter dependencies (e.g., spring-boot-starter-web, spring-boot-starter-data-jpa).
3. Observe how Spring Boot automatically configures various components without you writing any configuration code.
4. Try adding some custom configuration (e.g., setting database connection properties) and see how it interacts with autoconfiguration.

This exercise will give you a hands-on feel for how Spring Boot autoconfiguration works and how it simplifies Spring development.

9.2 Spring Boot CLI

Okay, let's talk about the Spring Boot CLI (Command Line Interface). This is a tool that can significantly speed up your initial development and prototyping with Spring Boot. It provides a way to quickly create and run Spring applications from the command line, often with minimal code.

So, what exactly *is* the Spring Boot CLI? It's a command-line tool that simplifies working with Spring Boot.

It allows you to:

- Initialize new Spring Boot projects: Quickly create project skeletons with the necessary dependencies and structure.
- Run Spring applications: Compile and execute Spring Boot applications directly from the command line.
- Execute Groovy scripts: Write Spring applications using Groovy, which can be more concise than Java, and run them using the CLI.

The Spring Boot CLI is particularly useful for:

- Rapid Prototyping: Quickly experimenting with Spring Boot features and building proof-of-concepts.
- Learning Spring Boot: Getting started with Spring Boot without the overhead of setting up a full project in an IDE.
- Scripting: Automating tasks related to Spring development.

Installation

The installation process varies depending on your operating system. You can typically use a package manager like SDKMAN! (for Unix-like systems) or download a distribution and set up your environment variables.

Key Features and Usage

Let's explore the main features of the Spring Boot CLI:

- spring init: This command is used to initialize new Spring Boot projects. It's similar to using Spring Initializr (the web tool) but from the command line. You can specify dependencies, project name, and other options.
  - Example: Creating a web application with Thymeleaf and Spring Data JPA:

Bash

```
spring init --dependencies=web,thymeleaf,data-jpa --name=my-web-app
```

  - This command will generate a basic Maven project with the specified dependencies and a src/main/java/DemoApplication.java file (or similar) containing a simple Spring Boot application.
- spring run: This command compiles and runs a Spring application from the command line. It's particularly useful for running Groovy scripts.
  - Example: Running a simple Groovy script:

```
Groovy
```

```
@RestController

class MyController {
```

```
@GetMapping('/')

String home() {

    "Hello from Spring Boot CLI!"

}

}
```

- Save this code as app.groovy and then run:

Bash

spring run app.groovy

- This will start a web server and you can access the greeting at http://localhost:8080/.
- Dependency Management: The CLI handles dependency resolution, so you don't have to manage your pom.xml or build.gradle directly when using Groovy.
- Groovy Support: The CLI has first-class support for Groovy, allowing you to write Spring applications in Groovy. Groovy can be more concise than Java, which can be beneficial for scripting and rapid prototyping.

Important Considerations

- While the CLI is great for getting started quickly, for larger or more complex projects, you'll typically want to use a full-fledged IDE (like IntelliJ IDEA or Eclipse) and a build tool like Maven or Gradle.
- The CLI's Groovy support is primarily for scripting and quick development. For production-level applications, Java

is generally preferred due to its stronger typing and tooling support.

Real-World Examples

- Prototyping a Microservice: You could use the CLI to quickly create a basic microservice with a few endpoints to test its functionality before integrating it into a larger system.
- Building a Data Processing Script: You could write a Groovy script using the CLI to perform a one-off data migration or transformation task.
- Demonstrating Spring Boot Features: The CLI can be a handy tool for showcasing Spring Boot capabilities in a concise way.

Practical Exercise

1. If you haven't already, install the Spring Boot CLI on your system.
2. Use the spring init command to create a few different Spring Boot projects with varying dependencies (e.g., a web application, a data access application).
3. Write a simple Groovy script that uses Spring Boot features (e.g., a REST controller) and run it using spring run.
4. Experiment with different CLI options and commands.

This exercise will give you a good feel for the Spring Boot CLI and its capabilities. Remember that while it's a powerful tool for certain scenarios, it's not always the best choice for all types of Spring development.

9.3 Spring Boot Actuator

Okay, let's discuss Spring Boot Actuator. This is a very useful feature that provides insights into your running Spring Boot application. It's like having a set of built-in tools to monitor and manage your application's health and performance.

So, what exactly does Spring Boot Actuator do? It exposes a set of endpoints (accessible via HTTP or JMX) that provide operational information about your application.

This information can be invaluable for:

- Monitoring: Checking the application's health, metrics, and other vital signs.
- Management: Performing administrative tasks, like shutting down the application or changing logging levels.
- Debugging: Getting detailed information to help diagnose issues.

Think of it as the control panel of your application, giving you a clear view of what's happening under the hood.

Adding Actuator to Your Project

To use Actuator, you need to add the spring-boot-starter-actuator dependency to your project.

Maven:

XML

```
<dependency>

    <groupId>org.springframework.boot</groupId>

    <artifactId>spring-boot-starter-actuator</artifactId>

</dependency>
```

Gradle:[1]

```
Gradle
```

```
dependencies {

    implementation
'org.springframework.boot:spring-boot-starter-act
uator'

}
```

Actuator Endpoints

Actuator provides a range of built-in endpoints, each providing specific information.

Here are some of the most commonly used ones:

- /actuator/health: Shows the health status of the application. It indicates whether the application is up and running correctly. It can also provide details about the health of specific components, like the database connection.
- /actuator/info: Displays arbitrary application information. You can configure this information in your application.properties or application.yml file.
- /actuator/metrics: Provides various metrics about the application, such as memory usage, CPU usage, HTTP request counts, and garbage collection statistics.
- /actuator/loggers: Allows you to view and modify the logging levels of loggers in your application.
- /actuator/env: Exposes the application's environment properties, including system properties and environment variables.
- /actuator/beans: Displays a list of all Spring beans in the application context.

- /actuator/mappings: Shows a list of all request mappings (URLs) in your application.
- /actuator/shutdown: Allows you to gracefully shut down the application. (This endpoint is disabled by default for security reasons.)

Accessing Actuator Endpoints

You can access Actuator endpoints via HTTP. The base path for these endpoints is /actuator. So, to access the health endpoint, you would typically use the URL http://localhost:8080/actuator/health (assuming your application is running on port 8080).

Here's an example of the response you might get from /actuator/health:

JSON

```
{

  "status": "UP"

}
```

This indicates that the application is healthy.

Customization

Actuator is highly customizable. You can:

- Enable/Disable Endpoints: By default, some endpoints are enabled, and some are disabled for security reasons. You can control which endpoints are enabled using configuration properties.

Properties

```
management.endpoints.web.exposure.include=* #
Expose all web endpoints

management.endpoints.web.exposure.exclude=env,bea
ns # Exclude env and beans endpoints
```

- Customize Endpoint Paths: You can change the base path and the paths of individual endpoints.

Properties

```
management.endpoints.web.base-path=/admin   #
Change base path to /admin

management.endpoint.health.path=/status   # Change
health endpoint path to /status
```

- Add Custom Information: You can add your own custom information to the /actuator/info endpoint.

Properties

```
management.info.app.name=My Application

management.info.app.version=1.0.0
```

- Secure Endpoints: You can secure Actuator endpoints using Spring Security to prevent unauthorized access.

Real-World Examples

- Monitoring Application Health: In a production environment, you can use the /actuator/health endpoint to monitor the health of your application and receive alerts if it becomes unhealthy.

- Collecting Metrics for Performance Analysis: You can use the /actuator/metrics endpoint to collect metrics like request latency and memory usage, which can help you identify performance bottlenecks and optimize your application.
- Dynamically Changing Logging Levels: You can use the /actuator/loggers endpoint to dynamically change the logging levels of specific loggers without restarting the application, which can be very helpful for debugging issues in production.

Practical Exercise

1. Create a Spring Boot application and add the spring-boot-starter-actuator dependency.
2. Run the application and access the /actuator/health, /actuator/info, and /actuator/metrics endpoints using a web browser or a tool like curl or Postman.
3. Customize the /actuator/info endpoint by adding your own application information in application.properties or application.yml.
4. Experiment with enabling and disabling different Actuator endpoints using configuration properties.
5. (Optional) Secure the Actuator endpoints using Spring Security.

This exercise will give you a hands-on understanding of how to use Spring Boot Actuator to monitor and manage your Spring Boot applications.

9.4 Spring Boot Starter Dependencies

Okay, let's discuss Spring Boot Starter Dependencies. These are a key feature that greatly simplifies dependency management in your Spring Boot projects. They're like pre-packaged bundles of libraries that you commonly need for specific tasks, saving you from the hassle of figuring out which individual dependencies to include and ensuring they're all compatible.

So, what exactly are Spring Boot Starters? They are a set of convenient dependency descriptors that you can include in your application. Each starter contains all the dependencies you need to get started with a particular technology or functionality.

Think of them as recipe kits for building your application. Instead of gathering all the individual ingredients (dependencies) yourself, you get a kit that contains everything you need in the right proportions.

Here's why Starters are so helpful:

- Simplified Dependency Management: You don't have to manually specify the versions of individual dependencies. Spring Boot manages this for you, ensuring compatibility.
- Reduced Boilerplate: You don't have to include numerous individual dependencies in your pom.xml (Maven) or build.gradle (Gradle) file.
- Increased Productivity: You can get started with a specific technology much faster, as you don't have to spend time researching and configuring dependencies.
- Consistency: Starters promote consistency across your projects, as they use a standardized set of dependencies.

Common Spring Boot Starters

Spring Boot provides a wide range of starter dependencies for various use cases. Here are some of the most frequently used ones:

- spring-boot-starter-web: This starter includes everything you need to build web applications using Spring MVC.

It includes:

- ○ Spring MVC
- ○ Tomcat (the default embedded web server)
- ○ spring-web (for basic web support)
- ○ Jackson (for JSON processing)

XML

```xml
<dependency>

    <groupId>org.springframework.boot</groupId>

<artifactId>spring-boot-starter-web</artifactId>

</dependency>
```

- spring-boot-starter-data-jpa:[1] This starter includes everything you need to work with JPA (Java Persistence API) for database access.

It includes:

- ○ Spring Data JPA
- ○ Hibernate (the default JPA implementation)
- ○ spring-jdbc (for basic JDBC support)

You'll typically also need a database driver dependency (e.g., for MySQL or PostgreSQL) along with this starter.

```
<dependency>

<groupId>org.springframework.boot</groupId>

<artifactId>spring-boot-starter-data-jpa</artifac
tId>

</dependency>

<dependency>2

<groupId>com.mysql</groupId>

<artifactId>mysql-connector-j</artifactId>3

</dependency>

` ` `
```

- spring-boot-starter-security: This starter provides everything you need to secure your Spring applications. It includes Spring Security, which is a powerful and highly customizable security framework.

XML

```
<dependency>

    <groupId>org.springframework.boot</groupId>


<artifactId>spring-boot-starter-security</artifac
tId>

</dependency>
```

- spring-boot-starter-test:[4] This starter includes all the dependencies you need for testing Spring applications. It includes:
  - JUnit Jupiter (for unit testing)
  - Spring Test (for integration testing)
  - Mockito (for mocking)
  - AssertJ (for fluent assertions)

```xml
<dependency>

<groupId>org.springframework.boot</groupId>

<artifactId>spring-boot-starter-test</artifactId>

<scope>test</scope>5

</dependency>

```
```

Note the `<scope>test</scope>` element, which indicates that these dependencies are only needed for testing and won't be included in the production application.

- spring-boot-starter-thymeleaf: This starter includes everything you need to use Thymeleaf as your template engine for building web views.

XML

```xml
<dependency>

    <groupId>org.springframework.boot</groupId>
```
```

```xml
<artifactId>spring-boot-starter-thymeleaf</artifa
ctId>

</dependency>
```

- spring-boot-starter-mail:[6] This starter provides support for sending emails.

XML

```xml
<dependency>

    <groupId>org.springframework.boot</groupId>

    <artifactId>spring-boot-starter-mail</artifactId>

</dependency>
```

These are just a few examples. Spring Boot provides many other starters for various technologies and use cases.

Real-World Example

Let's say you're building a simple REST API to manage a list of books. You would likely use the following starters:

- spring-boot-starter-web: To handle HTTP requests and responses.
- spring-boot-starter-data-jpa: To interact with a database (if you need to persist the books).
- spring-boot-starter-test: To write tests for your API.

By including these starters, you get all the necessary dependencies without having to specify them individually.

Practical Exercise

1. Create a new Spring Boot project using Spring Initializr or your IDE.
2. Add different Spring Boot starter dependencies to your pom.xml or build.gradle file.
3. Observe how Spring Boot automatically includes a set of related dependencies based on the starters you add.
4. Experiment with using the functionality provided by the starters (e.g., creating a simple web controller with spring-boot-starter-web, or interacting with a database with spring-boot-starter-data-jpa).

This exercise will help you understand the convenience and power of Spring Boot Starter Dependencies and how they can significantly speed up your development process.

Chapter 10: Best Practices and Design Patterns

So, you've learned the fundamentals of Spring, and you're ready to build real-world applications. That's fantastic! But simply knowing the syntax and features isn't enough. You also need to understand how to structure your applications well, optimize their performance, secure them properly, and make them easy to maintain and scale. That's what this chapter is all about.

10.1 Architectural Patterns for Spring Applications

Okay, let's talk about architectural patterns specifically in the context of Spring applications. These patterns are fundamental to designing robust, scalable, and maintainable systems. They're not just abstract concepts; they're practical blueprints that guide you in structuring your code and organizing your application's components.

So, what exactly are architectural patterns? They are proven, reusable solutions to common design problems in software architecture. They provide a high-level vocabulary and a set of best practices for organizing the different parts of your application and defining how they interact. Think of them as established roadmaps that help you navigate the complexities of software design and avoid common pitfalls.

Let's explore some of the architectural patterns you'll frequently encounter when building Spring applications:

1. Layered Architecture

This is one of the most fundamental and widely used architectural patterns. It organizes an application into distinct layers, each with a specific responsibility. This separation of concerns simplifies development, testing, and maintenance.

A typical layered architecture for a Spring application often includes these layers:

- Presentation Layer: This layer is responsible for handling user interactions and presenting data to the user. In a web application, this is often where Spring MVC controllers reside. Its core functions include:
  - Receiving and processing incoming requests from the user (e.g., HTTP requests).
  - Validating user input to ensure it's in the correct format and meets business rules.
  - Converting data between different formats (e.g., from a database entity to a JSON response).
  - Orchestrating the response to the user, which might involve selecting an appropriate view or returning data.
- Business Layer (or Service Layer): This layer contains the core business logic of the application. It defines the application's functionality and rules. It's responsible for:
  - Implementing business processes and workflows (e.g., order processing, user authentication).
  - Enforcing business rules (e.g., a user cannot place an order if their account is suspended).
  - Coordinating interactions between different data access objects to fulfill a business request.
- Data Access Layer: This layer handles communication with the database or other data storage mechanisms. It's responsible for:
  - Retrieving data from the database.
  - Saving, updating, and deleting data in the database.
  - Mapping between database records and the application's data objects (entities).
  - Handling database-specific exceptions.

Let's illustrate this with a more detailed code example.

Consider a simple online store application:

Java

```java
// Presentation Layer (Controller)

import
org.springframework.web.bind.annotation.*;

import java.util.List;


@RestController

@RequestMapping("/products")

public class ProductController {


    private final ProductService
productService;


    public ProductController(ProductService
productService) {

        this.productService = productService;

    }


    @GetMapping
```

```java
        public List<ProductDTO> getAllProducts()
{

            return
productService.getAllProducts();

        }



        @GetMapping("/{productId}")

        public ProductDTO
getProductById(@PathVariable Long productId) {

            return
productService.getProductById(productId);

        }



        @PostMapping

        public ProductDTO
createProduct(@RequestBody ProductDTO productDTO)
{

            return
productService.createProduct(productDTO);

        }



        @PutMapping("/{productId}")
```

```java
        public ProductDTO
updateProduct(@PathVariable Long productId,
@RequestBody ProductDTO productDTO) {

            return
productService.updateProduct(productId,
productId);

        }



        @DeleteMapping("/{productId}")

        public void deleteProduct(@PathVariable
Long productId) {


productService.deleteProduct(productId);

        }

    }



    // Business Layer (Service)

    import
org.springframework.stereotype.Service;

    import java.util.List;

    import java.util.stream.Collectors;



    @Service
```

```java
public class ProductService {


    private final ProductRepository
productRepository;


    public ProductService(ProductRepository
productRepository) {

        this.productRepository =
productRepository;

    }


    public List<ProductDTO> getAllProducts()
{

        return
productRepository.findAll().stream()

            .map(this::convertToDTO)

            .collect(Collectors.toList());

    }


    public ProductDTO getProductById(Long
productId) {

        return
productRepository.findById(productId)
```

```java
            .map(this::convertToDTO)

            .orElse(null);

    }



    public ProductDTO
createProduct(ProductDTO productDTO) {

        // Business logic (e.g., validation,
authorization)

        Product product =
convertToEntity(productDTO);

        Product savedProduct =
productRepository.save(product);

        return convertToDTO(savedProduct);

    }



    public ProductDTO
updateProduct(ProductDTO productDTO, Long
productId) {

        // Business logic (e.g.,
authorization)

        Product product =
convertToEntity(productDTO);

        product.setId(productId); // Ensure
correct ID
```

```java
        Product updatedProduct =
productRepository.save(product);

        return convertToDTO(updatedProduct);

    }


    public void deleteProduct(Long productId)
{

        // Business logic (e.g.,
authorization)

productRepository.deleteById(productId);

    }


    private ProductDTO convertToDTO(Product
product) {

        ProductDTO dto = new ProductDTO();

        dto.setId(product.getId());

        dto.setName(product.getName());

        dto.setPrice(product.getPrice());

        return dto;

    }
```

```java
    private Product
convertToEntity(ProductDTO productDTO) {

        Product product = new Product();

product.setName(productDTO.getName());

product.setPrice(productDTO.getPrice());

        return product;

    }

}


    // Data Access Layer (Repository)

    import
org.springframework.data.jpa.repository.JpaReposi
tory;


    public interface ProductRepository extends
JpaRepository<Product, Long> {

        // Custom query methods can be added here

    }


    // Model (Entity)

    import javax.persistence.*;
```

```java
@Entity

public class Product {


    @Id

    @GeneratedValue(strategy =
GenerationType.IDENTITY)

    private Long id;

    private String name;

    private double price;


    // Constructors, getters, and setters

    public Product() {}

    public Product(Long id, String name,
double price) {

        this.id = id;

        this.name = name;

        this.price = price;

    }

    public Long getId() {

        return id;
```

```java
        }

        public void setId(Long id) {

            this.id = id;

        }

        public String getName() {

            return name;

        }

        public void setName(String name) {

            this.name = name;

        }

        public double getPrice() {

            return price;

        }

        public void setPrice(double price) {

            this.price = price;

        }

    }


    // Data Transfer Object (DTO) - For
Presentation Layer

    public class ProductDTO {
```

```java
    private Long id;

    private String name;

    private double price;


    // Constructors, getters, and setters

    public ProductDTO() {}

    public ProductDTO(Long id, String name,
double price) {

        this.id = id;

        this.name = name;

        this.price = price;

    }

    public Long getId() {

        return id;

    }

    public void setId(Long id) {

        this.id = id;

    }

    public String getName() {

        return name;

    }
}
```

```java
public void setName(String name) {

    this.name = name;

}

public double getPrice() {

    return price;

}

public void setPrice(double price) {

    this.price = price;

}

}
```

In this more elaborate example:

- The ProductController handles HTTP requests for product management.
- The ProductService implements the core business logic (e.g., retrieving, creating, updating, and deleting products) and uses the ProductRepository for database access.
- The ProductRepository (using Spring Data JPA) handles the database interaction for the Product entity.
- We also introduce a ProductDTO (Data Transfer Object). This is a best practice to separate the data format used in the presentation layer from the internal data format (the Product entity). This improves flexibility and decoupling.

Benefits of Layered Architecture:

- Separation of Concerns: Each layer has a specific responsibility, making the code more organized and easier to understand.

- Maintainability: Changes in one layer are less likely to affect other layers, reducing the risk of unintended consequences.
- Testability: You can test each layer in isolation, making it easier to pinpoint and fix bugs.
- Reusability: Layers can be reused across different parts of the application or even in other applications.

2. Microservices Architecture

This architectural style structures an application as a collection of small, independent services. Each service is responsible for a specific business capability[1] and communicates with other services[2] over a network (typically using HTTP or messaging).

Instead of building a monolithic application where all functionalities are tightly coupled, you break it down into smaller, manageable units.

Spring Cloud provides a rich set of tools to support microservices development, including:

- Service Discovery (Eureka, Consul, etc.): Services can automatically register themselves and discover other services.
- API Gateway (Spring Cloud Gateway): A single entry point for clients to access the various microservices.
- Configuration Management (Spring Cloud Config): Centralized management of configuration for all services.
- Message Brokers (RabbitMQ, Kafka): Asynchronous communication between services.
- Circuit Breakers (Resilience4j): Handling failures and preventing cascading failures.

A real-world example:

Consider a complex e-commerce application. You could break it down into microservices for:

- Product Catalog Service: Manages product information.
- Order Service: Handles order placement and processing.
- Customer Service: Manages customer accounts and profiles.
- Payment Service: Processes payments.
- Shipping Service: Handles shipping and delivery.

Benefits of Microservices Architecture:

- Scalability: Each service can be scaled independently, allowing you to allocate resources efficiently.
- Flexibility: Different services can use different technologies and programming languages.
- Faster Development and Deployment: Smaller services are easier to develop, test, and deploy.
- Fault Isolation: If one service fails, it doesn't necessarily bring down the entire application.

Choosing the Right Pattern

The choice of architectural pattern depends heavily on the specific requirements of your application.

- For small to medium-sized, relatively simple applications, a layered architecture is often a good starting point. It's well-established and provides a solid foundation.
- For large, complex, and rapidly evolving applications that need to scale significantly and be developed by multiple teams, a microservices architecture might be a better fit.

It's crucial to carefully evaluate the trade-offs of each pattern, considering factors like complexity, scalability requirements, team size, and development speed.

Here's a practical exercise:

1. Choose a software application you are familiar with (e.g., a social media platform, a video streaming service, a ride-sharing app).
2. Identify the main functionalities or features of that application.
3. Consider how you might structure that application using a layered architecture. What would the responsibilities of each layer be?
4. If the application is large and complex, think about how you might break it down into microservices. What would the boundaries of each service be?

This exercise will help you develop your ability to analyze application requirements and choose an appropriate architectural pattern.

10.2 Performance Optimization Techniques

Okay, let's talk about performance optimization. This is a vital aspect of building efficient and responsive Spring applications. It's not just about making things "faster"; it's about using resources intelligently, handling load effectively, and providing a smooth experience for users.

So, why should we care so much about performance?

- User Experience: Fast applications are crucial for user satisfaction. Nobody likes waiting for pages to load or for actions to complete. A snappy, responsive application keeps users engaged and productive.
- Scalability: Well-optimized applications can handle more users and more requests without slowing down or crashing.

This is essential for applications that need to grow and handle increasing traffic.

- Resource Consumption: Efficient applications use fewer resources (CPU, memory, network bandwidth, etc.), which translates to lower operating costs and better overall system stability.

Let's explore some key performance optimization techniques that are particularly relevant to Spring applications:

1. Caching

Caching is a technique where you store frequently accessed data in a fast-access location (like memory) to avoid retrieving it from a slower source (like a database) repeatedly. Spring provides a powerful caching abstraction that simplifies implementation.

- @Cacheable: This annotation is your primary tool for adding caching. When you apply it to a method, Spring checks if the result of that method call is already in the cache. If it is, Spring returns the cached result; otherwise, Spring executes the method, stores the result in the cache, and then returns it.

Java

```
import org.springframework.cache.annotation.Cacheable;

import org.springframework.stereotype.Service;



@Service

public class ProductService {
```

```
@Cacheable("products")

public Product getProductById(Long id) {

    // Simulate a slow database retrieval

    System.out.println("Fetching product from
database...");

    try {

        Thread.sleep(1000);

    } catch (InterruptedException e) {

        Thread.currentThread().interrupt();

    }

    return
productRepository.findById(id).orElse(null);

    }

}
```

In this example:

- o @Cacheable("products") tells Spring to cache the
  result of getProductById() in a cache named
  "products."
- o The first time this method is called for a given id, the
  product is retrieved from the database, and the result
  is stored in the "products" cache.

- ○ Subsequent calls to getProductById() with the same id will retrieve the product from the cache, bypassing the database call.
- @CacheEvict: This annotation is used to remove entries from the cache. You'd typically use it when data changes, and the cache needs to be updated.

Java

```java
import
org.springframework.cache.annotation.CacheEvict;

import org.springframework.stereotype.Service;


@Service

public class ProductService {


    @CacheEvict("products")

    public void clearProductCache() {

        System.out.println("Clearing all products
from cache");

    }


    @CacheEvict(value = "products", key = "#id")

    public void evictProduct(Long id) {
```

```java
        System.out.println("Evicting product with
id: " + id);

    }

}
```

- ○ @CacheEvict("products") clears the entire "products" cache.
  - ○ @CacheEvict(value = "products", key = "#id") clears a specific entry in the "products" cache, identified by the id. The #id is Spring Expression Language (SpEL) to access the id method argument.
- @CachePut: This annotation is used to update the cache with the method's result. It *always* executes the method and then puts the result into the cache.

Java

```java
import
org.springframework.cache.annotation.CachePut;

import org.springframework.stereotype.Service;



@Service

public class ProductService {


    @CachePut(value = "products", key =
"#product.id")
```

```java
    public Product updateProduct(Product product)
{

        System.out.println("Updating product in
cache and database");

        return productRepository.save(product);

    }

}
```

- ○ @CachePut(value = "products", key = "#product.id")
  updates the cache with the result of updateProduct(),
  using the product's ID as the cache key.

To use these annotations, you also need to configure a cache manager. Spring provides adapters for various caching providers (e.g., Caffeine, Redis). Spring Boot often auto-configures a simple in-memory cache if you don't explicitly configure one.

2. Asynchronous Processing

For operations that are time-consuming and don't need to return a result immediately, asynchronous processing can significantly improve your application's responsiveness. Spring's @Async annotation makes it easy to execute methods in a separate thread.

```java
Java

import
org.springframework.scheduling.annotation.Async;

import org.springframework.stereotype.Service;
```

```java
@Service

public class EmailService {


    @Async

    public void sendOrderConfirmationEmail(String
email, String orderDetails) {

        // Simulate sending an email (this might
take time)

        System.out.println("Sending confirmation
email...");

        try {

            Thread.sleep(5000);

        } catch (InterruptedException e) {

            Thread.currentThread().interrupt();

        }

        System.out.println("Confirmation email
sent to: " + email);

    }

}
```

You also need to enable asynchronous processing in a Spring configuration class:

Java

```
import
org.springframework.context.annotation.Configurat
ion;

import
org.springframework.scheduling.annotation.EnableA
sync;


@Configuration

@EnableAsync

public class AsyncConfig {

}
```

When you call sendOrderConfirmationEmail(), Spring will execute it in a separate thread, allowing the main thread to continue processing other requests.

3. Database Optimization

Database interactions are often a major source of performance bottlenecks.

Here are some key optimization strategies:

Efficient Queries:

- Use indexes to speed up data retrieval.
- Avoid SELECT * and retrieve only the columns you need.
- Use appropriate JOIN clauses to minimize the number of queries.
- Analyze query execution plans to identify areas for improvement.

Connection Pooling:

- Use a connection pool (like HikariCP) to reuse database connections, reducing the overhead of establishing new connections for each request. Spring Boot often configures this automatically.

Batch Operations:

- If you need to perform multiple database operations (e.g., inserting many rows), use batching to execute them in a single database call, improving efficiency.

Lazy Loading (JPA/Hibernate):

- If you're using an ORM like JPA, use lazy loading to defer loading related entities until they are actually accessed. This can prevent unnecessary database queries.

Database Tuning:

- Tune your database server configuration (e.g., buffer pool size, query cache settings) for optimal performance.

4. Efficient Data Structures and Algorithms

Choosing the right data structures and algorithms is essential for performance, especially when dealing with large datasets.

- Use HashMap for fast lookups by key.
- Use HashSet for fast membership checks.
- Avoid inefficient sorting algorithms when possible.

- Consider using specialized data structures for specific tasks.

5. Profiling and Monitoring

- **Profiling:** Use profiling tools (like Java Flight Recorder or VisualVM) to identify performance bottlenecks in your code. These tools can help you pinpoint which methods are consuming the most CPU time or memory.
- **Monitoring:** Use monitoring tools (like Spring Boot Actuator) to track application metrics in real-time, such as request latency, memory usage, and garbage collection activity.

Real-World Example

Consider a social media application. You could use:

- Caching to store frequently accessed user profiles or recent posts.
- Asynchronous processing to handle tasks like sending notifications or processing image uploads.
- Database optimization techniques to speed up queries for retrieving user feeds or search results.

Practical Exercise

1. Create a Spring Boot application with a method that performs a slow operation (e.g., simulating a complex calculation or a time-consuming database query).
2. Implement caching using @Cacheable to improve the performance of this method.
3. Implement asynchronous processing using @Async to execute another slow operation in a separate thread.
4. Use Spring Boot Actuator to monitor the application's performance metrics (e.g., request processing time, memory usage). You can use a tool like a web browser or curl to access the Actuator endpoints.

This exercise will give you practical experience with performance optimization techniques in a Spring application.

10.3 Security Best Practices

Security in Spring applications isn't about adding a few lines of code at the end; it's about building security into your application from the ground up. It's a mindset and a series of practices that need to be followed throughout the development lifecycle.

Let's break down some essential security best practices:

1. Input Validation

This is the cornerstone of secure development. It's the principle of *never trusting user input*. Any data that comes from outside your application's control (whether it's from a web form, an API request, or even a file) should be treated as potentially malicious.

Why is this so critical? Because improper input validation is the root cause of many security vulnerabilities. Attackers often try to exploit weaknesses in how applications handle input to inject malicious code or manipulate the application's behavior.

Here's a detailed look at what input validation entails:

- Sanitization: This involves cleaning or modifying the input to remove or escape potentially harmful characters.
    - For example, in web applications, if you're displaying user-provided text in HTML, you need to escape HTML special characters (like <, >, and &) to prevent Cross-Site Scripting (XSS) attacks. XSS attacks occur when attackers inject malicious scripts into your web pages, which can then be executed by other users' browsers.
- Format Validation: This involves checking if the input adheres to the expected format.

- Examples:
  - Verifying that an email address has a valid structure (using regular expressions or libraries).
  - Checking if a date string matches a specific date format.
  - Ensuring that a phone number consists of only digits and has the correct length.
- Type Validation: Ensuring that the input is of the expected data type.
  - Example: If you're expecting a number, make sure the input can be parsed as a number and isn't a string.
- Range Validation: Checking if numerical input falls within acceptable limits.
  - Example: Verifying that an age value is within a reasonable range (e.g., between 0 and 120).
- Length Validation: Ensuring that strings don't exceed maximum lengths to prevent buffer overflows or database issues.

Whitelisting vs. Blacklisting:

Whitelisting: This is generally the preferred approach. It involves defining a set of allowed characters, values, or patterns and rejecting anything that doesn't conform. This is more robust because it's harder for attackers to find ways to bypass the validation.

Blacklisting: This involves defining a set of *disallowed* characters, values, or patterns and filtering them out. This is less secure because attackers might discover valid inputs that are not on the blacklist.

Spring provides some built-in validation mechanisms, but you should always implement your own robust validation logic, tailored to the specific requirements of your application.

Here's an example using Spring's validation annotations and handling validation results:

```Java
import org.springframework.http.HttpStatus;

import org.springframework.http.ResponseEntity;

import org.springframework.validation.BindingResult;

import org.springframework.web.bind.annotation.PostMapping;

import org.springframework.web.bind.annotation.RequestBody;

import org.springframework.web.bind.annotation.RestController;

import javax.validation.Valid;

import javax.validation.constraints.Email;

import javax.validation.constraints.NotBlank;

import javax.validation.constraints.Size;


@RestController
```

```java
public class UserController {


    @PostMapping("/users")

    public ResponseEntity<?> createUser(@Valid
@RequestBody User user, BindingResult
bindingResult) {

        if (bindingResult.hasErrors()) {

            StringBuilder errorMessage = new
StringBuilder();


bindingResult.getFieldErrors().forEach(error ->


errorMessage.append(error.getField()).append(":
").append(error.getDefaultMessage()).append("; ")

            );

            return
ResponseEntity.badRequest().body(errorMessage.toS
tring());

        }


        // Process the user (e.g., save to
database)

        // ...
```

```java
        return
ResponseEntity.status(HttpStatus.CREATED).body("U
ser created successfully");

    }

}


class User {


    @NotBlank(message = "Username is required")

    @Size(min = 3, max = 20, message = "Username
must be between 3 and 20 characters")

    private String username;


    @NotBlank(message = "Email is required")

    @Email(message = "Invalid email format")

    private String email;


    private String password;


    // Getters and setters (omitted for brevity)

    public String getUsername() {

        return username;
```

```java
    }


    public void setUsername(String username) {

        this.username = username;

    }


    public String getEmail() {

        return email;

    }


    public void setEmail(String email) {

        this.email = email;

    }


    public String getPassword() {

        return password;

    }


    public void setPassword(String password) {

        this.password = password;
```

}

}

- @Valid:[1] This annotation tells Spring to validate the User object based on the constraints defined in the User class.
- BindingResult: This interface holds the results of the validation. You can check it to see if any errors occurred.
- @NotBlank, @Size, @Email: These are standard validation annotations that define constraints on the username, email, and other fields.

2. Authentication and Authorization

These are the two fundamental processes that control access to your application:

Authentication: This is the process of verifying the identity of a user or a system. It's about answering the question, "Who are you?".

Common authentication methods include:

- Username/Password Authentication: The user provides a username and password. This is still the most common method, but it's crucial to handle passwords securely (see below).
- Multi-Factor Authentication (MFA): Adds an extra layer of security by requiring users to provide multiple verification factors[2] (e.g., password and a code from an authenticator app, or password and a fingerprint).
- OAuth 2.0: A framework that allows applications to obtain limited access to user accounts on an HTTP service without requiring the user's credentials. It's often used for "Sign in with Google" or similar functionality.

- JWT (JSON Web Token): A standard for securely transmitting information between parties as a JSON object. It's commonly used in RESTful APIs.

Authorization: This is the process of determining what resources an authenticated user is allowed to access and what actions they are permitted to perform. It's about answering the question, "What are you allowed to do?".

Common authorization methods include:

- Role-Based Access Control (RBAC): Assigning roles to users (e.g., "ADMIN", "USER", "EDITOR") and granting or denying access to resources based on those roles.
- Attribute-Based Access Control (ABAC): Defining access control policies based on attributes of the user, the resource, and the context (e.g., time of day, location).

Spring Security is the most powerful and flexible framework for implementing authentication and authorization in Spring applications.

Here's a simplified example of configuring Spring Security for basic authentication and role-based authorization:

```java
import
org.springframework.context.annotation.Bean;
```

```java
import
org.springframework.context.annotation.Configurat
ion;

import
org.springframework.security.config.annotation.we
b.builders.HttpSecurity;

import
org.springframework.security.config.annotation.we
b.configuration.EnableWebSecurity;

import
org.springframework.security.core.userdetails.Use
r;

import
org.springframework.security.core.userdetails.Use
rDetails;

import
org.springframework.security.provisioning.InMemor
yUserDetailsManager;

import
org.springframework.security.web.SecurityFilterCh
ain;


@Configuration

@EnableWebSecurity

public class SecurityConfig {


    @Bean
```

```java
    public InMemoryUserDetailsManager
userDetailsService() {

        UserDetails user =
User.withDefaultPasswordEncoder()

            .username("user")

            .password("password")

            .roles("USER")

            .build();

        UserDetails admin =
User.withDefaultPasswordEncoder()

            .username("admin")

            .password("password")

            .roles("ADMIN")

            .build();

        return new
InMemoryUserDetailsManager(user, admin);

    }


    @Bean

    public SecurityFilterChain
filterChain(HttpSecurity http) throws Exception {

        http

            .authorizeHttpRequests()
```

```
.requestMatchers("/public/**").permitAll() //
Allow access to /public/**


.requestMatchers("/admin/**").hasRole("ADMIN") //
Require ADMIN role for /admin/**

                .anyRequest().authenticated() //
Require authentication for any other request

            .and()

            .httpBasic(); // Use basic
authentication


        return http.build();

    }

}
```

- @EnableWebSecurity: Enables Spring Security's web security features.
- InMemoryUserDetailsManager: A simple, in-memory implementation of Spring Security's UserDetailsService (for demonstration purposes only; don't use this in production).
- SecurityFilterChain: This bean defines the security rules for your application.
- authorizeHttpRequests(): Configures authorization rules.
  - requestMatchers("/public/**").permitAll(): Allows access to any URL starting with "/public/" without authentication.
  - requestMatchers("/admin/**").hasRole("ADMIN"): Requires the user to have the "ADMIN" role to access any URL starting with "/admin/".

- ○ anyRequest().authenticated(): Requires authentication for any other URL.
- httpBasic(): Enables basic authentication.

Important Password Handling:

Never store passwords in plain text! Always use strong hashing algorithms (like bcrypt or Argon2) to store password hashes. Spring Security provides excellent support for password hashing.

3. Secure Communication (HTTPS)

Always use HTTPS to encrypt all communication between the client and the server. This prevents eavesdropping, where attackers can intercept and read sensitive data being transmitted.

You'll need to:

- Obtain an SSL/TLS certificate from a Certificate Authority (or use a self-signed certificate for development purposes).
- Configure your web server (e.g., Tomcat, which is often embedded in Spring Boot applications) to use HTTPS.

4. Protect Sensitive Data

- Encryption: Encrypt sensitive data both at rest (when it's stored in the database) and in transit (when it's being transmitted).
- Secure Storage of Secrets: Don't store API keys, database passwords, and other secrets directly in your code or configuration files. Use environment variables, secure configuration management systems, or dedicated secret management tools.

5. Regular Security Updates

Keep your Spring framework, Spring Security libraries, and all other dependencies up to date. Security vulnerabilities are discovered regularly, and updates often include crucial patches. Use a build tool (Maven or Gradle) to manage your dependencies and regularly check for updates.

6. Error Handling

- Avoid Exposing Sensitive Information: Don't include detailed error messages that might reveal information about your system's internals, database structure, or configuration.
- Log Errors Securely: Log errors in a secure location and avoid logging sensitive data in your logs.
- Provide User-Friendly Error Messages: Give clear and helpful error messages to the user without exposing technical details that could be exploited.

Real-World Example

Consider an API for a healthcare application. Security is paramount.

You'd need to:

- Use strong authentication (possibly with multi-factor authentication) to verify the identity of doctors and patients accessing the system.
- Implement fine-grained authorization to control access to patient records, ensuring that only authorized personnel can view or modify specific data.
- Encrypt all communication with HTTPS to protect patient data from interception.
- Securely store patient data in the database, using encryption and access control mechanisms.

- Regularly audit the application for security vulnerabilities and apply updates promptly.

Practical Exercise

1. Create a Spring Boot application with a simple REST API.
2. Implement basic input validation for a data submission endpoint.
3. Add Spring Security to your project and configure authentication with an in-memory user store.
4. Define different roles (e.g., "ADMIN", "USER") and restrict access to certain API endpoints based on these roles.
5. (Optional) Explore using JWT for authentication instead of basic authentication.
6. (Optional) Configure HTTPS for your application (this might involve generating a self-signed certificate for testing purposes).

This exercise will provide you with valuable hands-on experience in implementing essential security best practices in a Spring application.

10.4 Maintainability and Scalability Considerations

Okay, let's discuss two very important aspects of software development: maintainability and scalability. These aren't just buzzwords; they're crucial for building applications that can evolve over time and handle increasing demands.

Maintainability

Maintainability is all about how easy it is to modify, update, and fix your application. A maintainable application is like a well-organized toolbox – you can quickly find the right tool, make changes without breaking other things, and add new tools without cluttering everything.

Here are some key factors that contribute to maintainability in Spring applications:

Code Organization:

- Clean Code Principles: Follow principles like writing self-documenting code, using meaningful names for variables and methods, keeping methods short and focused, and avoiding code duplication. This makes your code easier to read and understand.
- Modular Design: Break down your application into logical modules or components. Each module should have a clear responsibility and well-defined interfaces. Spring's component model helps with this.
- Package Structure: Organize your classes into a clear and consistent package structure. This helps developers navigate the codebase and understand the relationships between different parts. For instance, you could have packages like com.example.service for your business logic, com.example.controller for your web controllers, and com.example.repository for your data access objects.

Dependency Management:

- Minimize Dependencies: Only include the dependencies you actually need. Unnecessary dependencies can increase the complexity of your application and introduce potential conflicts.
- Dependency Injection (DI): Use Spring's DI to decouple your components. This makes it easier to replace or modify dependencies without affecting other parts of the application. We've talked a lot about this already!

- Dependency Version Management: Use a build tool (Maven or Gradle) to manage your dependencies and their versions. This helps ensure consistency and avoids version conflicts. Spring Boot's Starter Dependencies are excellent for this.

Logging:

- Comprehensive Logging: Implement thorough logging throughout your application. Log important events, errors, and warnings. This makes it much easier to diagnose problems and understand the application's behavior.
- Structured Logging: Use a structured logging format (like JSON) to make your logs easier to parse and analyze.
- Log Levels: Use appropriate log levels (DEBUG, INFO, WARN, ERROR) to categorize your log messages.
- Log Rotation: Configure log rotation to prevent log files from growing too large.

Testing:

- Thorough Testing: Write comprehensive unit and integration tests to ensure that your code works correctly and that changes don't introduce regressions.
- Test-Driven Development (TDD): Consider using TDD, where you write tests before you write the actual code. This can lead to cleaner, more focused code.

Configuration Management:

- Externalize Configuration: Store configuration settings (like database connection details, API keys) outside of your code, typically in properties files, YAML files, or environment variables. This makes it easy to change settings without recompiling your application. Spring Boot's configuration mechanisms support this well.

- Configuration Profiles: Use Spring's profiles feature to define different configurations for different environments (development, testing, production).

Real-World Example (Maintainability)

Consider an e-commerce application. If it's designed with good maintainability in mind:

- Adding a new payment method (e.g., a new gateway) should be relatively easy because the payment processing logic is well-separated.
- Updating the look and feel of the website shouldn't require major changes to the business logic.
- Fixing a bug in the order processing logic shouldn't introduce new issues in the product catalog.

Scalability

Scalability is all about your application's ability to handle increasing workloads. This could mean more users, more requests, more data, or more transactions. A scalable application can grow to meet these demands without significant performance degradation or system failures.

Here are some key scalability considerations in Spring applications:

Statelessness: Design your application to be stateless whenever possible. This means that each request can be handled by any instance of your application. Statelessness is crucial for horizontal scaling, where you add more servers to handle increased traffic.

Load Balancing: Distribute incoming traffic across multiple instances of your application to prevent any single instance from becoming overloaded. Spring Cloud provides tools for load balancing in microservices architectures.

Caching: As discussed earlier, caching can significantly improve performance and reduce the load on your database.

Database Scalability:

- Read Replicas: Use read replicas of your database to handle read-heavy workloads.
- Database Sharding: Partition your database into smaller, more manageable pieces to distribute the load.

Asynchronous Processing: Use asynchronous processing (e.g., with Spring's @Async) to handle long-running tasks without blocking the main thread. This improves responsiveness and frees up resources.

Message Queues: Use message queues (like RabbitMQ or Kafka) to decouple components and handle asynchronous communication. This can improve scalability and reliability.

Microservices Architecture: As discussed earlier, this architecture can be very beneficial for scalability, as each service can be scaled independently.

Real-World Example (Scalability)

A social media application needs to handle a massive number of users and posts.

To scale effectively:

- The application might be designed to be stateless, so new users can be added as needed.
- A load balancer would distribute traffic across multiple servers.
- Caching would be used to store frequently accessed data like user profiles and recent posts.
- Asynchronous processing would handle tasks like sending notifications.
- A message queue might be used to handle background tasks like image processing.

Practical Exercise

1. Choose a simple Spring Boot application you've built.
2. Identify areas where you can improve its maintainability (e.g., code organization, logging).
3. Consider how you might make the application more scalable (e.g., by adding caching or asynchronous processing).
4. Implement some of these improvements and observe the impact on the application's performance and maintainability.

By focusing on maintainability and scalability from the beginning, you can build Spring applications that are not only functional but also robust, efficient, and able to adapt to changing requirements.

Conclusion

Throughout this book, we've embarked on a detailed exploration of the Spring Framework, starting with its core principles and progressing to more advanced topics. We began by establishing a solid foundation in fundamental concepts like Dependency Injection (DI) and Inversion of Control (IoC), understanding how these mechanisms empower us to write cleaner, more modular, and testable code. We then navigated the various approaches to Spring configuration, from traditional XML-based methods to the modern and efficient annotation-based style, equipping you with the skills to effectively define and manage your application's components.

We moved on to the intricacies of Spring MVC, learning how to build robust web applications, handle HTTP requests and responses, and work seamlessly with forms and data binding. We also explored diverse view technologies, providing you with the tools to present your application's data in a user-friendly manner. The journey continued with a deep dive into Spring's data access capabilities, from the lower-level JDBC abstraction to the powerful and convenient Spring Data JPA, simplifying interactions with databases and ensuring data integrity.

Furthermore, we addressed the crucial aspect of building RESTful web services with Spring, covering everything from designing RESTful APIs to handling JSON and XML, managing HTTP status codes, and implementing essential security measures. We emphasized the importance of testing, providing practical guidance on writing effective unit tests with JUnit and Mockito, as well as comprehensive integration tests with Spring Test, ensuring the reliability and stability of your Spring applications.

Finally, we culminated our exploration with a discussion of best practices and design patterns, covering architectural considerations, performance optimization techniques, security guidelines, and strategies for building maintainable and scalable applications. This section aimed to equip you with the knowledge to craft production-ready, enterprise-grade Spring solutions.

By now, you should possess a comprehensive understanding of the Spring Framework, enabling you to design, develop, and deploy sophisticated Java applications. You've gained the skills to leverage Spring's powerful features to tackle a wide array of software development challenges.

However, the field of software development is constantly evolving. The Spring Framework itself continues to grow and adapt, with new releases and features emerging regularly. Therefore, continuous learning is essential. I encourage you to stay updated with the latest Spring documentation, community resources, and best practices. Explore Spring Boot and Spring Cloud to further enhance your ability to build modern, cloud-native applications.

This book provides a strong foundation, but it's just the beginning of your Spring journey. The real mastery comes with practice, experimentation, and a commitment to continuous improvement. I wish you all the best in your future Spring endeavors!

www.ingramcontent.com/pod-product-compliance
Lightning Source LLC
LaVergne TN
LVHW081514050326
832903LV00025B/1486